RED
LETTER
DAYS

RED LETTER DAYS

By
Matt Pryor

Edited by
Ian King

Published by
Washed Up Books

Thank you:
Christine Michele

Chapters

9	Coma
23	Smells & Bells
31	Acronym Girl
41	The Object That I Adore
49	The Outbreak Of Theory
61	In The Library
67	Suburban Get Up Kids
75	Close To Home
85	Better Half
93	In The Doghouse
99	Live To Gig, Gig To Live
109	It's Dark Out Lately
121	Dollars To Deutschmarks
135	Virgin Herb
143	The Company Dime
157	Land Yacht
171	Sustenance
179	The Dunder Chee
189	Shabu Shabu
203	Every Double Life
209	Red Letter Days
217	I'll Catch You

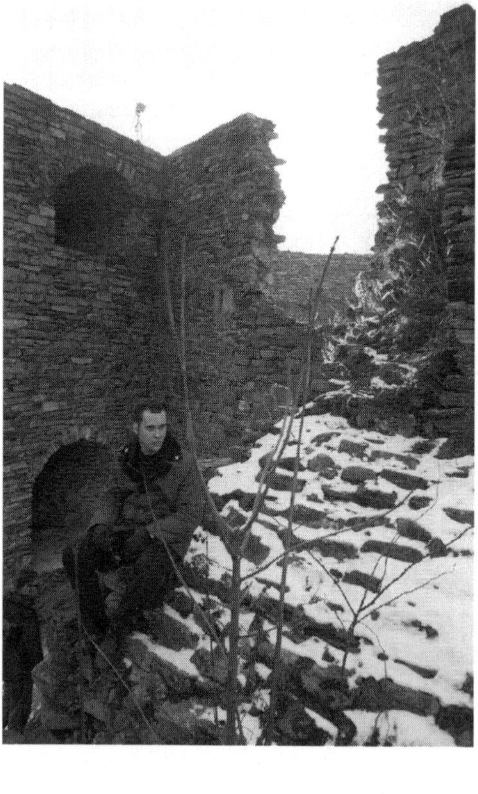

Coma

I am doubled over in pain, rolled into a ball beneath a desk in the offices of the Johnson County Community College in Overland Park, Kansas. I am only twelve years old but am not attending my sixth grade classes today. My mother has brought me to the college, where she works as a counselor, either because she actually believes that I am sick or she doesn't have time for my bullshit. I fake being sick a lot. My brother and I transferred to a—*gasp*—public elementary school in the middle of the year and I'm having a hard time. My parents have just divorced, and though this changes nothing about my father's generous paycheck, for some reason we can't afford private school anymore. That place wasn't any better, it was just more Christ-like to call me a faggot there than at this secular den of academic sinners.

I am a young metalhead, a white-trash poseur because I actually come from money. The one outlier in my record collection is the *Pump Up The Volume* soundtrack. That film about misfits really speaks to me. That and *Heathers*, except for the domestic terrorism. Damn, Christian Slater really had us pegged there for a minute. Though my glam metal heroes don coifs of gravity-defying spectacle, Catholic school dress code won't allow boys to have hair past their collars, so I have a sort of mini-mullet. Business in the front, Christian Mingle in the back. At least I can grow it out now. At my new school I have befriended another aspiring headbanger, a proper dirtbag with locks down to the middle of his back. It is within a week of meeting him that this strange illness takes hold of me.

I don't recall how the pain started, whether it was a slow build or an instantaneous gut punch. I just remember rolling around on the floor, moaning, embarrassing my mother in front of her coworkers. She probably brought me here so I couldn't Ferris Bueller it, or sit on the couch at home and watch game shows and sitcom reruns all day. I am in actual agony but getting little sympathy. I am the boy who cried wolf and cannot be trusted.

I am so thirsty, I drink whatever liquid I can get my hands on. Within minutes this causes a panic in my bladder so urgent I actually contemplate urinating on the floor like a dog. With great determination I rise to walk to the bathroom, doubling over, my abdomen screaming. I shuffle, slow as paint dries, my arms around my midsection, down a hall that feels like it must be miles long. Don't worry, I'm not going to go into detail about what happens in the stall. Let's just say it is impressive, if you're keeping score of things like that. This brings slight relief of the abdominal pressure and I make it back to the desk and fall asleep on the floor.

After mother's work ends we stop off at the drug store, or maybe the grocery store or pizza parlor. It's one of the three. I'm kind of in and out of reality at this point. One thing is crystal clear: I make it to the soda machine and get one each of the six different cans of soda. My thirst is insatiable and this Caligulan amount of corn syrup and synthetic flavoring is gonna do the trick, I think. One of the flavors is grape, and none of them are diet. That's important for what happens next.

Back home, I pour all six cans together into a plastic pitcher, the kind you put lemonade or iced tea in at a picnic and stir with a wooden spoon. Over the next half hour I consume all sixty-four ounces of this strange brew while sitting in my room listening to records by Pretty Boy Floyd or Electric Angels, or maybe Hanoi Rocks. Something isn't right. I run to the bathroom and immediately start to vomit. Needless to say, it is abundant...and purple because of the grape. It knocks the wind out of me and I go pass out in my bed.

I awake sometime in the middle of the night drenched in sweat. The pain in my stomach seems worse somehow. I call out for my mom but she's asleep. I slowly make my way over to her bedroom door and knock as loud as my weak body will allow. It's enough to wake her. She says I should take a bath. I do, and am then wet and in pain, followed by freezing and in pain. This is January in Kansas City, and the tile floor might as well have been made out of Ice-nine, freezing my whole body solid. Aching, I get dressed and make it back to my bed.

When I wake again I am screaming for my mother. She is visibly irritated, certain that this is a really elaborate act to get out of going to school. Doesn't matter, I am hallucinating. I start to tell her that I saw two figures, Mickey Mouse and Tina Turner, but they are gone now. I frantically explain to her that she needs to bring me Mickey Mouse and Tina Turner. That is going to make the pain stop. This is finally enough to convince her that something is actually wrong. She calls the hospital and they are sending an ambulance.

Upon the news that we are going to the hospital, I apparently look perfectly fine walking to the closet to get dressed. I no longer appear to be in pain at all. This all gets recounted to me later, because I have blacked out and do not remember anything about those moments. Frustrated and suspicious of my seemingly miraculous recovery, my mother calls off the ambulance. She's gonna put me to bed and I'm gonna sleep it off or something. As soon as she hangs up the phone and I start to head towards my bedroom, I take a wrong turn and promptly roll down the entire flight of stairs.

I wake up briefly as I am loaded into an ambulance on a gurney. Then I black out again. When I finally come-to proper, I am on my back in a hospital bed in the ICU. Things come into focus and there are people around me in scrubs. They are pleased that I am conscious. I look down and there are some sort of pods adhesively affixed to my hairless chest. They haven't shaved me, I am twelve. A gloved hand puts a spoon to my mouth. I expect something sweet but it's just crushed ice, an attempt to hydrate me. Disappointed by the ice, I ask what's going on. All they tell me is that I've been out but it's gonna be okay now. "Did my brother do this?" I ask them. They laugh and I go back to sleep.

I am stable but still in the ICU, and here's what I've learned: I've been in a diabetic coma. They have not told me for how long. I assume it was a few hours at most but no one in my family can remember. My pancreas, whatever the hell that is, has given up the ghost. Done-zo, kaput.

This means I am officially diagnosed with what is currently known as "juvenile diabetes" but eventually will just be called Type 1 diabetes. Apparently this broken pancreas thing makes something that's called insulin that regulates the sugar in your blood. The what? Sugar in your blood that comes from food. Ok...so what does that mean? It means I am now dependent on self-administered synthetic insulin to manage my blood sugar. This insulin is synthesized from pigs. Great, I am dependent on a porcine serum to stay alive.

I'll need to give myself injections of this insulin several times a day and I'll need to monitor what I eat and adjust the insulin accordingly. Everybody else's pancreas does this for them but mine is fucking useless, unfixable, and the whole disease has no cure. My understanding is that a normal, not-broken pancreas maintains a blood sugar level between 80 and 120. I do not know what these numbers represent. Grams? Ounces? Kilos? Regardless, when I came into the hospital my blood sugar was around 900, thus the coma. This all slowly sinks in. Well, it's not very eloquent, but this pretty much fucking sucks, am I right? I am right.

I am spending another night in the ICU for observation. The beds are separated by floor-to-ceiling curtains to give the illusion of privacy. The kid behind the curtain to my right was hit by a celebratory stray bullet on New Year's Eve, poor bastard. He is watching the movie *Willow* at quite the volume on the TV and VCR cart that they've wheeled into his area. When the film ends he screams "WILLOW! WILLOW!

WILLOW!" incessantly for about five minutes until a nurse arrives to rewind the tape so he can watch it again. This happens every two hours. I can't believe he isn't sick of this movie yet, I'm sure as shit done with it. I will never watch *Willow* again, traumatized by this child's incessant wailing.

After my stint in the ICU they put me in a recovery room. This is your basic hospital room, but with an extra bed for one of my parents. My education about the maintenance of this disease starts today and, since I am a minor, this includes the education of my parents as well. It's pretty simple. Fundamentally I need to learn the difference between the food groups, most importantly carbohydrates. Insulin eats sugar, and sugar comes from carbs. This is a not-very-accurate simplification but that's how I explain it to myself. I have to manually give myself injections of two different types of insulin. The first is slow-acting, which I am to take once a day, ideally at the same time every evening. This becomes my baseline, kinda like maintaining a buzz at a party. It's just rolling along under the surface.

Now the second kind is the wild card. It's fast-acting, though not that fast. Essentially whenever I want to eat carbohydrates I need to take this insulin thirty minutes before I eat, and adjust the amount based on the number of carbs I'm going to ingest. Different carbohydrates are absorbed by the body at different rates, so I need to take that into consideration as well. I interpret this to mean I can still eat whatever the fuck I want as long as I take enough insulin. Though this is technically true, there will be consequences down the line for that sort of living. Diabetes is a slow-acting, degenerative disease. Since I am a child, and therefore bulletproof, I am not worried about the long-term consequences.

Besides the minimum of four injections a day—one for the baseline and one that's fast-acting for each of my three meals— there is also blood sugar testing. I must wound the tips of my fingers several times daily in order to draw blood like a masochist and place it on a strip inserted into a small machine.

It looks like a TV remote. It takes two minutes for the machine to tell me my blood sugar level. This number represents the balance of sugar to insulin in my blood, thus blood sugar. "Blood glucose," technically, but you can fuck right off with that shit. I am to aim for that normal level between 80 and 120. The more I injure myself for science, the tighter control I will most likely have. My fingers ache. They are weak and full of holes, and they will be for the rest of my life.

Here's the thing about blood sugar: too high and you feel sluggish, and then nauseous, and then eventually you hallucinate and end up in a coma (see previous story). That takes a bit of time and can be corrected with more insulin, chasing the dragon of what that hypothetical candy bar is doing to your body. Too low, on the other hand, and that's a different, more immediate problem. Some, like Julia Roberts' character in *Steel Magnolias*, can go so far as to have seizures. I'm one of the luckier ones. When my sugar is around 80, I start to feel like something is off. Around 60 my stomach growls and I get ravenously hungry, like a stoner with the munchies. Lower than that and I instinctively panic, my heart races and I break out in a sweat. I will, in a loss of self-control, inhale any chips, chocolate, ice cream, candy, juice or soda that isn't nailed down. Like the heart-shaped life points in Zelda, if I hit zero, if I run out of sugar in my blood, I will die. This, so far, has not happened.

Kids who are old enough to give themselves injections are taught how to use a contraption called a "rocket." Essentially it's a spring-loaded piece of plastic that is kinda shaped like a space phallus housing a syringe that, at the press of a button, is plunged into my skin. More precisely, my body fat. Insulin doesn't go into your veins like fun drugs. It gets absorbed into your body slowly, and thus must be injected into the fatty parts of your arms, legs, stomach, and ass, I guess, but I don't wanna mess with that.

The thing is, even at this point needle technology has come a long way and these needles are very, very small. If done correctly the injection is somewhere between a pinch and no pain at all.

But the psychology of that trigger finger, hovering over that button, not knowing the pain it could inflict, is torturous. Plus, the brute force of a needle tip being catapulted into my flesh causes me to bruise. I don't use the rocket for long, instead switching to manual injections, primarily in my stomach.

The doctors give my parents syringes filled with salt water so they can give themselves fake insulin shots. I guess this is to make them more sympathetic to what I'm going to have to do every day, but who cares. I don't want their sympathy. I'm not exactly a big fan of them right now anyway. I was pretty angry and stubborn before the coma, and I'm certainly not going to take any pity from these two. This is my burden, alone, and we're gonna keep it that way.

I've already made my mind up that it's not gonna kill me right now. It's not terminal cancer. It's a pain in the ass but so is life, so I'm just gonna fucking deal with it. I will learn later that this is a common trait in Type 1 diabetics. We tend to be a bullish, independent lot. I assume it's a control thing. Having lost control of our bodies in this way, we attempt to find any part of our lives that we can actually have command over.

I meet with a nutritionist, and she talks about counting carbs and adjusting insulin. I absorb about half of what she says. They send me to a meeting of other teenagers afflicted with this sugar sickness. These losers are fucking lame. They have real Christian youth group, fake-positivity vibes. Barf. It's a total turnoff. Don't try to tell me that this is normal. It's not normal, my body has failed me. It sucks but I'll deal with it. I don't need to be in a sharing circle. I don't need to be reassured that I'll still get to play sports. I don't play sports, I'm a sedentary teenager who wants to read metal magazines and listen to records. These fucktwits can take their self-help bullshit and shove it up their cheerful asses. I want to go home. I finally get to go home.

The standard-issue diabetes maintenance kit goes as follows: Minimum four syringes in the 50-100 cc range. Two bottles of insulin, one fast-acting and one slow. Cooling system for insulin, which must be held at refrigerator temperature, usually an ice pack or frozen gel. Blood sugar meter, blood sugar test strips, lancing device to draw blood from finger. Disposable lancet to insert in lancing device for maximum skin penetration. Alcohol wipe to sterilize finger, plus gauze or more alcohol wipes to dispose of excess blood. Finally, something to use in case of emergency low blood sugar.

Glucose tablets taste like chalk, and glucose gel is literally prescription cake icing. You really can just carry a small piping bag from the grocery store. After much trial and error I have come to depend on fruit leather, Stretch Island brand specifically. It's essentially a hippie fruit roll-up, nothing but natural sugar. I carry a minimum of six and take one whenever my sugar hits 80, two at 70, three at 60, etc. I've never needed more than six in my regular day-to-day. These are the weapons I carry at my side anywhere I go, day or night, rain or shine.

I am back at school. My parents have done some reconnaissance, informing my teacher and the principal of my current condition. I am to be given special consideration if I need to leave the class or am having low blood sugar. We must inform my fellow students as well. The weird girl with the pigtails and glasses tells me that she understands, her cat has diabetes. Great. I have a cat disease managed by pig insulin. This is torturous, just give everybody the memo and let's move on. This is my deal, unless something goes off the rails you'll never hear about it from me ever again. Can you please, for the love of God, just leave me alone.

The following summer I am sent to "diabetes camp." It's an overnight camp that lasts for one week each year. They bring in special counselors with some medical training and all the campers are Type 1. We do outdoor bullshit all week. Hiking, swimming, canoeing, that sort of crap. We all wear fanny packs with our *d'betus* kit and comfortable shoes. We have campfires but we don't make s'mores for obvious reasons. We sleep in one-room cabins and are bitten by mosquitoes. Bathing in cold-water communal showers, hanging our suits up on the line. Real folksy boy scout shit. It is my own personal hell.

These losers are worse than the *diabeteen* support group. They are all life-positive and outdoorsy. There are a few other loners but we never form an alliance. I haven't yet figured out that the enemy of my enemy is my friend. Every night our cabin listens to Metallica's *...And Justice For All* on cassette for some reason. This is to lull us to sleep. It is an odd soundtrack choice for this task. The boom box is set to an almost inaudible volume, as if a barely perceptible version of "Harvester Of Sorrow" is any less bombastic.

Every night at precisely 2:00 a.m. we are awakened, sometimes violently, by the counselors. We all have to check our blood sugar in the middle of the night. I never do this at home. Maybe it's different for other folks, but when my blood sugar level drops as I slumber, my racing heart rate wakes me up pretty quickly. This jarring practice makes it difficult to get back to sleep, and since we wake with the sun each morning I doubt I get more than a few hours of rest every night.

These supposedly medically trained counselors leave a lot to be desired. One evening we're scheduled to have a communal dinner of grilled meat tubes and watermelon. Since said meat tubes are a quick cook we are instructed to go ahead and take our fast-acting insulin. Remember, it takes thirty minutes to kick in, so the timing of the meal has to be pretty exact. Needless to say, the lighting of the fire takes longer than expected. The thirty-minute window passes...then forty minutes...then forty-five. Several people are starting to get low blood sugar since they now have an overabundance of insulin in their systems. The counselors are unprepared for this sort of emergency. They have not brought any glucose tablets or gel, certainly not any fruit leathers. Instead we descend on the watermelon like ravenous wolves, covering our faces with sticky red flesh and seeds. It is a blood bath but we survive. I'll never like watermelon after this.

On the last night of camp we are allowed to sleep outside. We climb into the back of a very large tractor-drawn trailer that has been dismounted and docked in front of our cabin on top of a hill. We talk some but mostly just stare at the night sky and drift away under the stars. When we awake we are still in the wagon, but we are now at the bottom of the hill. Perplexed, we assume this was some sort of practical joke played by the counselors. We come to find out that in executing said joke our overlords lost control of the wagon, which went careening down the hill unmanned and full of sleeping teenagers. It was caught moments before crashing violently into the wall of the next cabin over. We had slept through the whole thing, mere moments from serious injury or death. I shudder to think at the repercussions of that particular lawsuit.

At the end of the week I am extracted and driven back to civilization. I am neither excited nor relieved about this. Camp sucked only slightly worse than regular life, mainly because of the mosquitoes. I say nothing the whole ride home.

Within a year of my diagnosis my mother remarries. My new stepfather is significantly older than she is, but this doesn't bother me. That he and I are wholly incompatible will become bothersome, but it isn't an issue we need to address yet. They met at a support group. I am encouraged to go to the teen version of this support group. I am not in favor of this idea. I reluctantly agree to go because it might be better than the therapist I am being forced to visit twice a month.

Here's a tip: using textbook psychobabble on an angry teenager whose only real mission in that hour on the couch is to piss you off isn't gonna change any hearts or minds. If you ask "How does that make you feel?" one more time I will cut out your heart and feed it to wolves. I *feel* like this whole exercise is pointless and I'm not gonna talk about it anymore with the likes of you. I did get to fight the bastard with a foam bat in a role-playing exercise and got a good crack at his skull. That was the most therapeutic breakthrough we had.

19 The teen support group is within walking distance from my house and in the same strip mall as Gomer's Chicken. I can get a small paper bag of fried gizzards for a dollar before a meeting. Hooray for little victories. This group isn't like the Ned Flanders-esque diabetic teen support group bullshit. These are people like me, angry and disenfranchised. They are actually pissed that their worlds are fucked up and broken, and are not trying to cover that up. This is a refreshing worldview to encounter, one not unlike my own. I start to make actual friends with some of these people. I will eventually play music with some of these people. Stranger still, some of what they talk about is making sense, it's getting through to me. I actually want to come back.

Over the next year, this group becomes my family. Not my blood relatives, who I want nothing to do with. In that smoke-filled and coffee-stained room they are my chosen kin. New people come and go, but there is a core group of us that attend week in and week out.

The summer before I am to start high school we decide to move back to my old neighborhood, to a bigger house and a different parish. Soon this meeting won't be within walking distance. I worry that I may have to say goodbye to this group for good. An event is suggested. An all-nighter, a lock-in. The kind of thing normal, less traumatized teens do.

There are two new girls in the group who will be attending. One of them is older and kinda terrifying, and the other is a year younger than me. She smokes like a chimney and swears like a sailor. I am in love. When the night comes we are all dropped off. Our skeptical parents are put at ease, since even though we are all degenerates we are going to a support group event.

Mostly we just sit around and talk. Some smoke, some play music. The local public access radio station has a punk rock show. They decide to play a newly released album by a Seattle trio in its entirety on the air. It's that good. I have already heard a few songs from *Nevermind* several times, having recorded the previous week's show on cassette. Hearing it in its entirety we all sit in silence and listen to what seems like our own lives being sung back to us. It's like nothing we've ever heard.

As the evening carries on and people start to tap out, drifting off to sleep on the linoleum floor, I get to talking with the smoking girl. She's here because she got put in rehab when her psychopath father read her diary. She had tried going to the proper adult support group for stuff like that, but the creepy older men made her uncomfortable. So she ended up here with the other age-appropriate fuckups.

For some reason that is lost to time, we climb on top of a soda machine. We sit up there and talk for hours. I am inappropriate sometimes but she forgives me. Eventually we lean in close and bring our lips together. This is the first time I kiss Honey White. An explosion goes off in my brain and I am absolutely sure in that moment that she is the only person I will ever love. She, reasonably, isn't so sure.

After that night, we make the move to the posh side of Gregory Street, into a mini mansion. Mom's married up. Honey White and I are mere blocks from each other, but it feels like an ocean divides us. I attend the support group only when I can get a ride from either of my parents or one of the few in my misfit brotherhood who has a car. I see Honey White around less and less. I am slowly coming to terms with the fact that she is already the one who got away. I put on my polo shirt and my pleated slacks and make my way to my first day of Catholic high school. Hoo-fucking-ray.

This school is for fascists. The male dress code used to be any shirt with a collar and slacks, but they've since tightened the rules so that boys can only wear solid colors. The female population must wear identical Catholic schoolgirl jumpers, the kind they sell at Halloween stores. Their skirts can be no more than three inches above the knee. The man in charge of maintaining this dress code is the vice principal. He brings potential offenders into his office to measure their skirt lengths by hand. Fuck that guy.

Another caveat to the boys' outfits is that undershirts cannot have visible print on them. A budding sociopath who is soon to be my only friend in the school is suspended for wearing a Brainiac shirt with "Fuck y'all, we're from Dayton" under his uniform, but a football player merely gets detention for coming back from spring break with a "Silly faggot, dicks are for chicks" tee. The hypocrisy of this place is astounding. In the future I will refer to it as a prison and claim I would never return unless it was to set the building on fire. For now, on the first day of school, I only hate it as much as I hate everything else.

Freshman orientation is about what I expected in this new hell, but I meet a couple of other outsiders, an aspiring lawyer and a classically trained pianist. The pianist and his best friend attended a Lutheran grade school, and it seems odd that they would end up at a Catholic high school. I guess there are a handful of Jewish students in attendance as well.

It turns out that Honey White also went to the same Lutheran grade school as the pianist, and his best friend actually dated her when they were younger. It is through them that I am reunited with my true love. Again, she is not so sure. She's got some more living to do before she settles down, and this will prove difficult for me to accept. But for now all is well and right in the world. This is the first time I am happy since the coma. The universe has brought her back to me.

Smells & Bells

I am on my knees, genuflecting, my hands folded in prayer, attempting desperately not to fall asleep. Maybe if I put my head in my hands like a weeping widow I can get away with it. My mother gives me a stiff elbow to the arm and a momentary scowl before turning back to the altar. This is the homily, either the most interesting or painfully boring part of the mass. It's the part of the show when the priest riffs on what today's teachings are and what's going on in the world. He's like a stand-up comic who gets no laughs or applause. It's a strange custom, to end the speech in silence followed by a song. Years later at my stepfather's funeral I have to stop myself from applauding after the eulogy. We have a different customary response in my line of work.

I stare at the ornate and enormous chandeliers that hang stories above us and daydream about swinging from them like a monkey. St. Peter's isn't a cathedral but it looks like one. Its architecture is similar to the great churches of Europe. The windows are stained glass, we are surrounded by candles, and the choir serenades us from their loft. My mother sang in this choir when she was pregnant with me. She thinks that's why I'm so musical, but I'm pretty sure it's more hard work on my part than divine intervention. Behind the altar is an enormous series of interconnected paintings depicting angels, saints, Mary and baby J all with glowing halos backlighting their heads. The Tabernacle where the body and blood are stored is solid gold, or appears to be anyway, and in front of that is a solid marble altar where the priest is washing his hands.

I was baptized here. We started going to confession before I was old enough to understand what it meant, and I was forced into the job of altar boy in the fourth grade. The other priest's servants and I would steal communion wafers and wine from the storage closet backstage, marveling at but never touching the elaborate costumes of the priesthood. They dress so plain during the day, all black with a white collar, that they are almost unrecognizable in their robes. I wonder who does their holy dry cleaning, and does the dry cleaning solvent need to be blessed as well, the way holy water does?

Back in second grade, for my first communion my parents debated about which bottle of red wine tasted most like communion wine and gave me a glass the night before the ceremony. My mom would have had a better grasp on that particular bouquet since my dad rarely went to mass. I would protest this when my brother and I were forced to attend and he wasn't, but eventually came to the conclusion that if my two options are church or watching football I'd rather be in church. I wouldn't say it's a good people-watching spot, but the communion line is where it's at to see and be seen in our parish. You can feel the judgment when a member of the party is absent, including my father. Even at this young age I can tell we are a homogeneous lot, the only person of color being the refugee from somewhere in South America that we're supposed to be raising money for.

Tithing baskets are passed person-to-person down the length of the pew. That's a lot of loot, I think to myself. I'm pretty sure I could nick a fiver but I never try. Once a month my parents put a blue envelope in the basket like a Hallmark card. This is our tuition to the elementary school attached to the church. By funneling the money through the tax-exempt house of worship they can count it as a donation on their taxes. It's a pretty good hustle. Separation of church and state my ass.

Somewhere around third grade I start to have issues with the concept of heaven. The church doesn't talk about heaven and hell much, it has more of a post-Vatican II sort of vibe. They don't talk about a theoretical cloud city or even the judgmental waiting room of purgatory. It's just one word, "forever." "What does 'forever' mean?" I ask teachers and priests. *It means for all time.* "Well, what the hell does that mean?"

I just can't wrap my mind around it. "What do we even do there?" *You do whatever you want, forever.* "So, play Nintendo all day, I guess? But I'll eventually get sick of that most likely, what do I do then?" *You won't get sick of it, you'll be in heaven.* "What kind of an answer is that? Also, how do you know this even exists? Has anyone ever come back and described it? Would that be a ghost or an angel or what?" I am told to take a seat, my query going unanswered. Even at this young age the lack of logic is frustrating. I'm starting to wonder if this is all bullshit.

This will eventually lead me to a sort of agnostic humanism. I don't know one way or the other if there is a god. I do believe there is an energy to the universe, I just don't think anyone can actually explain it with certainty. I do believe, I have to believe, that humanity in the end will find its way. As of the writing of this book, however, my faith in humanity is tested daily. I'm not anti-religion because I've seen it work for people. My grandmother was very devout, and I saw how her faith helped her when she was dying. As long as you're not hurting anyone but yourself I don't really give two fucks what you believe in. You do you. It's when you start imposing your beliefs on other people that I get upset, especially when those beliefs are contrary to the foundations of your faith. By all accounts, the J Man seems to have been a pretty righteous dude, one who wouldn't force his will on anyone but rather lead by example. He's a lot like the Grateful Dead. It's not the band that's bad, it's the followers that really ruin it.

Side note: This analogy does not hold weight with many of my friends in the punk rock community, nor would a younger me have bought into this theory. But I've softened in my old age, and if you strip away all the noodling bullshit The Dead have actually got some decent songs.

My growing distrust in the logic of the faithful is exacerbated by the supposed followers of the church. My mother's interpretation of this particular brand of Catholicism is one of social justice, taking care of the poor, feeding the hungry, that sort of shit. She continues to practice this flavor of worship even when the congregation gets a lot more conservative during the Bush years. The church does outreach and fundraisers, and I am not aware of much abortion talk, though I am probably too young to even know what that is. The supposed sin of homosexuality isn't really brought up because it isn't really in the mainstream. No, the true crusade is against music.

During the satanic panic of the 1980s, St. Peter's, like every other Christian denomination, starts to become suspicious of heavy metal. I am a budding young metalhead and I am not swayed by the argument that Judas Priest is trying to get their fans to kill themselves with subliminal messages. However, the Danzig song "Possession," which starts with backward masking and erupts into a scream of agony before the band kicks in, scares the ever-living shit out of me. Besides devil worship everyone seems to be particularly obsessed with sex. A speaker comes to our class and recites the lyrics to Guns N' Roses' "It's So Easy" as if doing a poetry reading. It is hilarious. I am really just into the music, not the misogyny and devil worship. Even at a young age I can see that this stuff isn't serious and is all done for shock value.

In school we go to mass every Wednesday in our white polo shirts and blue slacks. The girls wear the traditional Catholic schoolgirl jumper and attempt to try out occasional boy-toy era Madonna jewelry to no avail. I try to grow my hair long but not past the collar. I beg and beg to get my left ear pierced. Not the right ear. Everybody knows that means you are gay, and having them both pierced means you actually want to be a girl. This is '80s elementary school logic. I finally convince my mom to let me go to the mall and get it pierced at a Claire's Boutique knockoff tchotchke shop, but I can only wear a barely visible stud.

I desperately wanted something that hung low, maybe the Dr. Feelgood caduceus or the *Appetite For Destruction* cross with the skulls. Nope to both. Probably not because they were incredibly gaudy but because of the skulls. My mother forbids me from wearing any clothing or accessories that feature human bones. Do you have any idea how hard it is to find heavy metal T-shirts that don't have skulls? Or satanic imagery? Or scantily clad large-breasted cartoon women? I am not left with many options.

There is a store in the suburbs called Xanadu that sells heavy metal T-shirts and posters. I have my dad drop me off there whenever he and my brother go shopping for baseball cards at the nearby mall and I spend hours browsing but am never able to buy anything. I finally sneak two supposedly inoffensive shirts by my household censorship board. One has Mötley Crüe's *Theater of Pain* album cover on it, with a pretty visible pentagram on the forehead of the tragedy mask which my mom overlooks. The other is the version of the classic G N' R crest with the tagline "Guns and fucking Roses" removed for polite society. It still has pistols on it, but violence is apparently fine with the censorship board, as long as there is no sex or human remains.

During this time I also get really into The Doors. This is before the Oliver Stone movie comes out, but getting into them isn't too far of a logical leap after seeing The Cult on MTV. I read *No One Here Gets Out Alive* and *Riders On The Storm* and am just fascinated by this brooding dark-spirited man on the cover of the books. My requisite dirtbag jean jacket has a back patch of Jim Morrison surrounded by flames. I don't know how this idolatry and witchcraft makes it past the dress code. Ironically, I would come to really despise everything that he represented on a professional level. I never wanted to be the unreliable performer that might vacillate between complete inebriation and total brilliance. I've softened on him now, though. He was just a kid.

Some of the teachers at my school are nuns, but not the kind you're thinking of. I don't get whacked across the knuckles with a ruler every time I get an answer wrong or make an inappropriate joke. These sisters wear brown habits and some of them even play guitar. Kinda like Maria in *The Sound Of Music*. They are usually the religious studies instructors, or sometimes teach Sunday school classes, which are an ingenious way to keep kids who can't shut the fuck up out of mass. A lot of the other teachers are men. Confirmed bachelors, you might call them, who are often the harsher, stricter type. Maybe they are trying to control us because of something they don't like about themselves?

The priest who baptized me and gave me my first communion, who kinda looked like Wilford Brimley, passes away. He's replaced by a younger priest who drives a Camaro and has a sign over his reserved parking spot that says "Don't even think about parking here," the implication being that God is watching. I think he's pretty cool, as priests go.

I bring him up because he's an anomaly to me. Why would a younger person go into this line of work? I'm having a hard time believing any of this shit, so why is he, a seemingly smart and progressive guy, going along with all this illogical dogma? He gives a sermon about faith, this mystical, magical, irrational way of thinking. I struggle with this. I have faith in many things, but I don't have faith in this. Certainly not blind faith. I still think that's ridiculous.

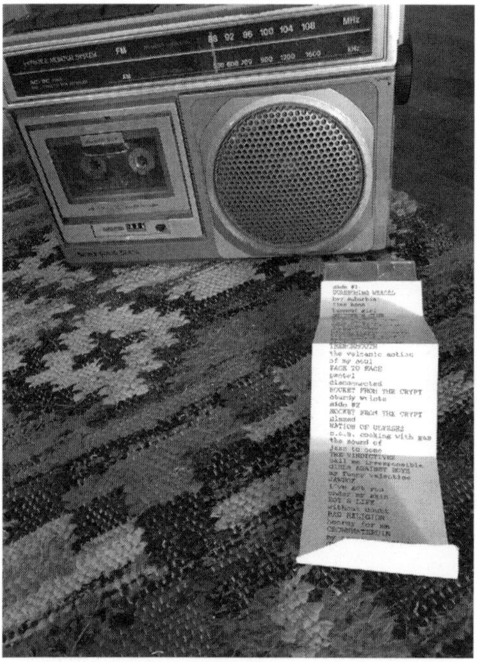

Acronym Girl

One of the attendees in the support group is a girl three days younger than me who uses an acronym for her name. It's actually her initials, but she's added an extra letter to make the whole conceit make sense. She's way cooler than me, listens to better music, and goes to a more enlightened school. It's one of those post-hippie academies for rich kids where they call the teachers by their first names and are allowed to take smoke breaks. She's not rich by any stretch of the imagination, so I have no idea how she affords to go to that school. Her father is a mailman and her mother is a starving artist, not exactly a trust-fund scenario.

We start to meet up outside of the group, but not in a romantic way. I'm not her type. She's more into the thrill-seeking skateboarder at her expensive school. He barely acknowledges her and treats her like shit when he does. She's in love. Above her bed she's got a subway poster of the Red Hot Chili Peppers all wearing socks on their penises, and another of the nude twin women from that Jane's Addiction album cover before it got censored. She's the one who first turned me on to the punk rock show on the local public radio station. We listen to her cassettes. At this point I still don't know much about punk. I think of it as sort of metal adjacent, but quickly learn that it's very much its own thing.

There's a concert coming to town, the first of its kind. Lollapalooza, an all-day experience featuring several of the bands we've heard on the punk rock show. One morning we wake before dawn to catch the bus to the mostly abandoned downtown mall to wait in line for tickets. We're not the only ones, the queue stretches around the block.

When the day comes, the concert itself turns out to be a mostly standard festival experience. No shade, expensive but bad food and drink, a lot of downtime between bands. I have to request a meeting with the medical staff so that I can bring in my insulin syringes. I also want to go to their offices whenever I take an injection. Nobody wants me shooting up in public, especially not this crowd, they might get the wrong idea. I also need to alert them about what to do if I have low blood sugar and this all goes to shit, which is entirely possible if I am out in the sun all day. I have a MedicAlert bracelet but I never wear it. I've started playing guitar and the chain bangs on the strings when I play.

Jane's Addiction, the headliner and owner of the festival, finally has a hit on the radio after years of touring and building a counterculture fan base. They come from LA and definitely have some glam influences, but with much more of an art-school aesthetic. It's still hedonism, all that sex, drugs and rock 'n' roll bullshit, but with a heavy emphasis on being original and odd. The dreadlocked Perry Farrell spasms as the ultra-goth Dave Navarro uses a vibrator to manipulate his guitar tone. They're like a dog whistle to every angry, misunderstood teenager.

I am taken aback by the amount of people that are here. I didn't really think about the size of this event, only that I wanted to attend as much as Acronym Girl. Are there really this many people that feel the way that I do, like nobody understands them? Unfortunately, no, that's not the case. This band, and even the festival itself, are already far enough into the mainstream that this audience is filled with the kind of people who have mocked me for being different. They apparently don't see the irony in being a fan of a band that celebrates individuality. I guess irony or self-reflection isn't this crowd's strong suit. Plus, this is an outdoor event in the summer. For a lot of folks here this is just something to do during a normally boring time of the year.

Acronym Girl's father picks us up after the concert in a Ford Econoline van that he bought to transport large paintings that her mom shuttles to galleries but never sells. He lovingly dotes on his daughter, but not in an overbearing way. This sort of affection is foreign to me. I wonder if it's a Latino thing. Then I wonder if that sort of thinking is problematic. They drop me off at home. Acronym Girl and I agree to meet up tomorrow for poetry.

There are a handful of coffee shops in town. None of them are sleek or decorated with reclaimed wood and Edison light bulbs. No, these are '90s coffee shops, which means thrift store furniture, shitty local art and, honestly, pretty bad coffee. We've started going to one on the Boulevard, where all the authentic Mexican restaurants are in town. This formerly abandoned building with a small stage is hosting an open mic poetry slam. Keep in mind that this was an era before that term became a punch line. Acronym Girl gets up to read a poem she's written. It's as heartfelt and painful to listen to as any teenager's diary, but I'm impressed that she got onstage and read it. I could never do that, I think to myself.

There's one guy, who goes by Black, who reads his work in the traditional style, not in the over-exaggerated "slam" style of the day. He reads slowly, pausing for emphasis, letting the beautiful words sink in. To this day, he's the only poet I've ever liked. He didn't carry himself with arrogance, he had a regular job and wasn't starving for his art, he just genuinely took joy from language.

Black invites Acronym Girl to read at another event he's hosting at a different makeshift coffee shop above a bookstore in the tavern district of Kansas City. After the poorly attended event we are invited back to Black's apartment with the other wannabe literati of our day. Black's apartment is a simple affair, the one standout being a Replacements poster on his fridge signed by the man Mr. Westerberg himself. The inscription reads "Glad you got to meet me. –Paul." Hilarious, I think to myself. Black's roommate is the only person I've met who has actual acid flashbacks. I've seen it happen. His eyes glaze over mid-sentence, and moments, sometimes minutes, later he's back, having no idea what just happened. His younger days must have been a wild ride.

Now in my older years I tend to look back on this moment with suspicion. Why did these adult men want to hang out with us kids? But at the time I thought we'd been allowed past the velvet rope and into the most exclusive club in the world.

I decide to try writing myself. I start journaling but am fearful of it being read by my mother, so I find myself censoring the words that come out of my brain. Eventually, at Acronym Girl's encouragement, I develop the courage to read at one of Black's events, but I decide to perform a song instead. I had been playing drums but you can't really write songs on that instrument, so I switched to guitar. I have a rudimentary understanding of the guitar but have figured it out enough to craft songs and learn some simple covers. There's no chance in hell that I could begin to understand the tablature featured in the metal-centric guitar rags but, luckily, punk rock requires very little musical virtuosity to play. It's one of the genre's superpowers and it's a game changer for me. Just knowing that songwriting is possible and that you don't have to be Yngwie Malmsteen to make music is a huge relief.

There's another band on the bill, an acoustic trio called The Young Johnny Carson Story, so I tell myself that my music won't be an outlier. Armed with my mother's ancient nylon string acoustic guitar, I am shaking with panic but find a way to get through a song I composed and the Pixies' "Wave Of Mutilation." The small audience applauds politely but I feel like I'm gonna vomit. Fuck that, I'm never doing that again.

The thing is, even though I'm terrible and terrified, I am still encouraged. These adults know that the will to perform is the first step toward actually being a performer. The same way the will to write or compose is the first step to becoming a writer or composer. They see that will in me, even though it scares me to death. They congratulate me, tell me they liked what they heard and that I should be proud of myself, knowing this was my first time performing. I am a bit taken aback, I'm not really used to praise. Looking back, I wonder where I'd be if they hadn't been so supportive of me in that moment. I'm still not comfortable with praise. "I can't take a compliment" is a true statement in one of the most popular lyrics I've written. If I hadn't gotten support then, I might not have ever tried performing again. How different my life would have turned out.

Acronym Girl introduces me to a local band called Mongol Beach Party. They have a jazzy, funky, weird party vibe and I'm here for it. Eventually their drummer will become a good friend and collaborator of mine. They are playing at an all-ages club, which I will come to find out are places for either Christian conversion or illicit drug consumption and heavy petting. Either way, it turns out my folks won't let me go to that show.

The next time they play is at Spirit Fest, a yearly concert at the WWI memorial, so we go to that instead. The other band Acronym Girl really wants to see is called Kill Whitey. They play an aggressive punk and grunge fusion, and their lead singer is a powerhouse. She wears kneepads because she drops to the ground so much during their performances. Their band name makes me a little uncomfortable though, which I think is the point. The college town alternative radio station has its own stage which features Kill Whitey and several bands from Lawrence. We watch Mongol Beach Party play early on the main stage. They are a little more palatable for the normies.

There's a strange vibe afoot. *Nevermind* has just broken and suddenly polite society has been made aware of a violent practice among the crowd at shows. This is the pit, of course, but the media has taken to calling it "moshing." I had thought moshing was that odd circle dance Scott Ian did when Anthrax played, his take on Angus Young's head banging. But nobody consulted me on the name.

Regardless, the pit is perfectly safe as long as everyone follows proper etiquette. The rules are simple: if someone falls down you pick them up, if someone crowd surfs you don't let them fall, and if someone stage dives you catch them and pass them back like a human joint. You do not use this medium to take out your bottled rage or meathead machismo on other people. But since popular culture is evolving and this style of dancing is becoming mainstream, more people are participating and doing it poorly. Plus, the security here has no idea what the fuck is going on because an out of control pit looks like a riot.

During Kill Whitey's set, Acronym Girl tells me she's going into the pit. Fuck that, not me. I'm a coward at regular shows, I'm not going anywhere near that violent group of rednecks and jocks. She calls me chicken but asks me to hold her backpack. I hang out back by the soundboard, next to the record store pop tent that I will work at in future years (I'll be paid in store credit, which is fine because that's where my money would go anyway).

The police doing security decide that things in the crowd have gotten out of control and pepper spray the entire pit. Acronym Girl comes running back to me, screaming for the love of her eyes. I give her a water bottle and she attempts to wash the poison from her face. Between tears and Dixie cups of festival water she gets it together enough to walk out. I think it's a gross overreaction, but honestly I wasn't in the melee so I don't know if it was warranted. The event makes the local news, it becomes a show of legend.

Acronym Girl meets Honey White through our mutual support group. When Honey White and I start dating I wonder if Acronym Girl is jealous, but I honestly don't think so. If anything, I'm jealous of the relationship that the two of them come to have. They both seem pretty independent without me, and I want to be the common link that joins them. This is not the case. They have friends in common at the local arts high school, including a former boyfriend of Honey White who is a kleptomaniac and dresses like Edgar Allan Poe. I would be jealous of him if he weren't very gay. Not sure how they ever dated in the first place.

Our Mutual Best Friend comes into the picture around this time. He's encouraged to come to the support group. He hates his parents, too, so it might be a good fit. We are a motley crew, the four of us. We'll go to various all-night diners around town and drink coffee and debate for the sake of debating. Our Mutual Best Friend is particularly good at this, and will take positions that I know he doesn't believe in just for the conflict. He would be a master debater if he ever went to school.

I've also started playing in a band with yet another member of the support group. Take A Joke is just that. The singer is a hippie who has named his car Amy Rae after one half of the Indigo Girls. The drummer is the older brother of a girl I went to Catholic school with who always scared the shit out of me. He and I trade off between drums and guitar. The bass player, the one from the support group, is kind of the leader of the band. He really ties the room together. We make a demo cassette called *Bicycles For Afghanistan* after the Vonnegut novel *Cat's Cradle*. I still have it. Not my best work.

Take A Joke plays a lot of backyards, kind of the St. Peter's and St. Elizabeth's Parish gig circuit, I guess. I am by far the youngest person in the band. The others are all either seniors in high school or have already graduated. These slackers talk about but never attend university, they are the definition of Gen-X. The bass player is the exception, he's very smart and motivated. He goes to the same college prep magnet school that Honey White will eventually attend after trying out the arts high school. I take note of the other guys' unwillingness to work and internalize it. They have a lot of time for drinking, smoking and complaining about life, but they never seem to do anything about their apparent unhappiness. I'm pretty sure that's not how I want to conduct myself.

One day Acronym Girl tells me she's shipping off to a hippie boarding school in Arizona. Again, I have no idea how she can afford this. I guess her folks must have starved themselves so that their daughter could have such privileges. I'm surprisingly fine with it, mainly because of my obsession with Honey White. She gives me a hug and kisses my cheek. It's the most intimate we've ever been and it's incredibly uncomfortable for me.

The Object That I Adore

I am a bit much. Codependent, they call it. I'm only sixteen years old, but that's really no excuse. My obsession with this girl is becoming a problem.

My love isn't unrequited. She does care about me, but is also seemingly more aware that we are, in fact, children. I would marry her today and run off together, but she's a little more levelheaded about it, and my behavior is starting to push her away. We break up and make up more times than I can count during our high school tenure. During a year in which we go to the same art school, she dumps me for a Ren Faire re-enactor who wears puffy pirate shirts to school. At one point she leaves me for Our Mutual Best Friend. Talk about kissing your sister.

I get my driver's license as soon as I am able, and the 1991 Honda Civic that becomes my de facto whip becomes our liberator. I'm the only one in our small group with a car. Our Mutual Best Friend left his on Bannister Road when it died, Honey White doesn't have a license yet, and neither does her sidekick. I hold an unbalanced amount of power in our collective friend group but I don't exercise any of it. I become everyone's chauffeur and I do it with glee. I want to be needed more than anything else.

Our first real "date" is to go with Acronym Girl to Memorial Hall in Wyandotte County to see the Chili Peppers with Smashing Pumpkins and Pearl Jam opening. I proudly display my Mother Love Bone shirt that I ordered out of a catalog and judge the plebes at this show. They don't know Mother Love

Bone, they don't even know who Pearl Jam is yet. Inevitably they will, but for now they are my little secret.

Rounding out this trip is a girl who keeps a pot-bellied pig in her laundry room. Well, she does for a few months, until it gets into the detergent and moves on to the great hog farm in the sky. Honey White and Girl with the Pig go off to their seats while Acronym Girl and I are on the floor. I got our tickets before I met Honey White—otherwise we'd be sitting together. Acronym Girl wants to get in the pit and crowd surf. I remind her that the last time she did that she got pepper sprayed during Kill Whitey at Spirit Fest. She doesn't care, she's gonna do it anyway.

I stand at the edge of the pit trying to simultaneously watch both the show and my friend to make sure she isn't trampled to death. It's early days for the mainstreaming of our underground and there's a heavy jock contingent here to see the Peppers. They seem to be less savvy about the rules of the pit and Acronym Girl is dropped during her crowd surfing session. She hits her head on the concrete floor and is helped up by a kindly purple-haired gentleman in a leather jacket. He walks her back to me and they start talking, flirting. I try to ask if she's injured but she ignores me. She's got stars in her eyes, and not from the fall.

After the show we meet up with Honey White and Girl with the Pig and they talk to Acronym Girl all the way to Chubbies Diner about the purple-haired guy. She says nothing about her fall or her likely concussion. I'm beyond jealous but say nothing. We roll into the Chubbies parking lot and find a couple mid-coitus on the hood of a Ford pickup. They pay us no mind as we try to move soundlessly through the lot to the front door of the diner.

Chubbies is your standard 1950s-themed diner, but it's before the Tarantino renaissance. The barstools and booths are covered in vinyl and Formica. The floor tiles are black-and-white checkerboard and the walls are adorned with black-and-white photos of Bill Haley and Ritchie Valens. The jukebox is filled with 45s by Buddy Holly and Chuck Berry among others.

Ever since the significantly more hip diner, Louise's, burned down under mysterious circumstances we've made Chubbies our haunt. We are the worst, often ordering one bottomless cup of coffee for the table and nothing else. I'm going through my *Reservoir Dogs* refusing-to-tip phase so I'm an even bigger asshole than the rest of the table. Post-gig, though, we actually order food because we need calories to offset the adrenaline drop. Finally we stop talking about the purple-haired guy and switch gears to the next show we're going to at Memorial Hall. I'm even more excited about this one, we're going to see fucking FUGAZI.

It's impossible to overstate the impact that Ian and Guy and Brendan and Joe have on my life even at this young age, especially at this young age. Their ethos and musical adventurousness becomes the foundation of both my songwriting and my humanity. Fuck Catholic school, I learn how to be a good person from *Repeater*. I will copy their lyrical cryptology, writing songs with verses obtuse enough that people never seem to know what they are actually about. It's like decoding a message in a bottle every time you learn the actual meaning of one of their songs. Sometimes when you sing words you don't really hear what they are. Most people don't really care, I think. But I do. I care a lot.

Weeks later, the show is packed. There were no advance tickets so everyone must wait in line. With the Ticketmaster service fee the tickets are ten dollars, which doesn't bother me but violates the band's strict five-dollar show policy. They are none too pleased about this development and say so from the stage, berating the venue and the promoter, but saving their most poisonous arrows for Ticketmaster itself.

The band asks to have the house lights turned on so they can see the crowd. Their stage lighting is two minimalist construction site work lights, and their attitude is that we're all in this together so we should all be able to see each other. For one song the house lights beam and the massive crowd is exposed. We're on the first upper level, about six feet above the floor. During the song the club turns the house lights off, defying the band's wishes. So the boys turn off the two stage lights, plunging the entire room into darkness as they strum the opening chords of "Blueprint" from muscle memory. At this point everyone on the first upper levels including Honey White and myself jump onto the floor and rush the stage, emboldened by the band's defiance.

Rumor has it that after the show the band's road manager got a gun pulled on him by the owner of the venue. Apparently he didn't like being told what to do by East Coast elites, let alone punks. Regardless, this is the fixed point in time when I notice a change. Sure, Nirvana was already on TV, and the jocks at school had started wearing combat boots and wallet chains, but this was over three thousand people who for the most part were on the same page.

In the coming years the rise of grunge and then pop punk will put our little island of misfit toys on the map. Soon others will be drawn to these shows because of the aggression in the music, not because of the meaning in the words. They say that primitive villages all started to collapse when they reached one hundred and fifty residents. Inevitably at that point they needed structure and leadership, and power ultimately leads to corruption. You could say the same thing about our little community, and I'm starting to see the frayed edges.

Our Mutual Best Friend and I started off as enemies. We met at Girl with the Pig's house one evening and initially bonded over our shared love of *Kids In The Hall*. He had taken some Mini Thins and was buzzing from the low-grade speed that was in style at the time. We could have been friends, but we also both shared a deep desire to be with Honey White. When I ultimately won that battle we became rivals. When she dumped me for the Ren Faire dipshit we found a common enemy and became fast allies.

He fights with his parents and is kicked out of the house regularly. On one occasion I drive all the way across town to the South Side to pick him up. We commune in Honey White's kitchen with her mother. They chain smoke and we all try to figure out what he wants to do, where he wants to go. Eventually he makes a call to a friend that I have never met and they decide to meet at Winstead's. I drive us there for our traditional one cup of coffee for four people, and we wait.

Over in a booth in the corner is a tormentor from my school who also went to grade school with Honey White. She was a tormentor back then as well. She and her abusive boyfriend are arguing, and their yelling causes enough commotion that they are asked to take it outside. Out in the parking lot he slams her head with the door of his car. Our server calls the cops, but nonetheless the tormentor gets into the car, dazed, driving off with the creep. A different car pulls up and Our Mutual Best Friend leaves the table and heads out into the night. All I know is that he and his friend are gonna go chase a tornado, and that we won't see him for a couple of days.

I've been terrified of tornados since I was a kid. During one such event in my youth, my parents decided we would hole up in the finished basement of their best drinking buddies' house. Even though the sirens were blaring my dad went on a beer run. I spent the next twenty minutes panicking, terrified he wasn't gonna make it home. Since then, I don't fuck with tornados. As soon as that weird hue falls over the neighborhood my heart starts to race. It's like someone put a green filter over the entire city and it's eerie as hell. *Please start raining, I'll pray, a thunderstorm would be much preferred.* But sometimes the sirens wail and we rush down to the basement and I shake uncontrollably.

I am, by some estimations, a coward. Besides the tornado thing, I don't fuck with heights, planes or roller coasters. Even as I'm writing this, I've never been on a roller coaster. The appeal is as foreign to me as a distant language, I know people dig it but I don't get why. You do you, though. I'm not here to yuck your yum, but I have no interest in terrifying myself on purpose. Life is scary enough on its own.

The aerophobia hasn't manifested itself yet, but will eventually become so crippling that I'll opt to take the train whenever possible. For a while I will have to get wicked drunk to get on a plane and pass out. If I wake up before takeoff, I recite the serenity prayer over and over like a mantra as the plane leaves the ground. That's probably the best thing I got from that support group. "The serenity to accept the things I cannot change, the courage to change the things I can, and the wisdom to know the difference." On an airplane I can't change anything and that's why it's so terrifying to me. That, and being in a submarine that could fall out of the sky.

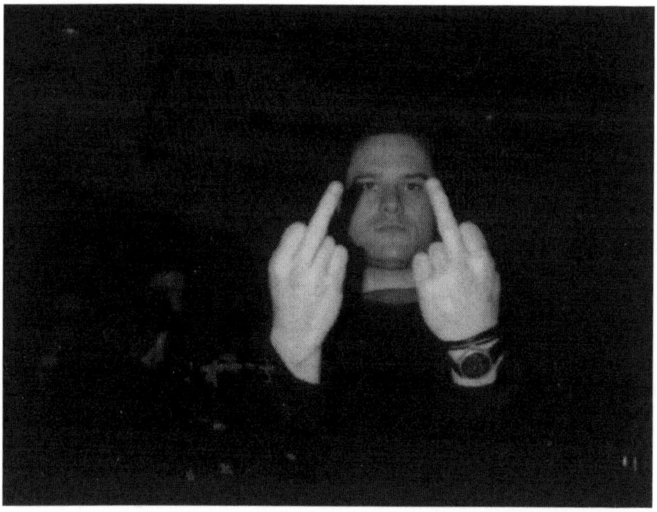

The Outbreak Of Theory

I am in a mathematical hell. Even at seventeen I know in the very marrow of my bones that I will never have to solve for X once I get out of this institution. I don't dislike numbers, but none of this theoretical bullshit is going to help me calculate the walk-out potential of a show or factor cost of goods sold to budget a merch order. There is plenty of projection when planning a tour but very little is concrete, let alone accurately solvable.

I'll spend the rest of this seemingly endless, tortuous hour sketching in the margins of a notebook. Not doodles or even comic strip characters. Not band logos or skulls. I'm constantly drawing and redrawing the most advantageous way to pack all of my new band's gear into the van.

I now carry a guitar in a "noise" band called Secular Theme. It's music for people who don't enjoy melody or song structure. We all wear oversized black suits and skinny ties like an amateur middle-class *Reservoir Dogs*. Our singer flails his arms around and swings a homemade microphone fashioned out of a landline telephone run through a distorted amplifier. He sometimes plays the saxophone. He does not know how to play the saxophone. We are rarely on a proper stage but are a commanding presence on the floor of a coffee shop or a basement. We are a whirling dervish of a band and it's fun as hell.

I can play the guitar in a fairly rudimentary manner but mostly I find ways to make it wail with feedback. I take the back plate off a thrift store Stratocaster copy and rake my pick over the springs, causing cacophonous reverb. I assault the instrument with the base of my hand as if to punish it. I pull the neck, bending the notes and ultimately knocking the whole fucking thing out of alignment. What does it matter? I'm using it more as a weapon or an instrument of torture anyway.

I have bought a 1969 Ford Econoline van with a manual choke and a complete lack of power steering from our drummer's dad. What kind of Tetris will maximize the use of the vehicle's limited space? Our current collection of amplifiers is small, but the drums don't have cases. This makes for a particularly precarious problem since the drums themselves are both fragile and, well, round. One day we will be able to put everything into oversized but uniformly square road cases, sturdy stackable coffins, but these cost a bit of cheddar so they are off the table for the time being.

Said drummer is a dirtbag. A skateboarding, spray-painting, drug-taking thief who could have played himself in the movie *KIDS*. He's only fifteen but he's the best drummer I know, and we can practice at his house. Sometimes the dirtbag's best friend will come over, he's a decent drummer, too. The two of them are hooligans, often disgusting and always juvenile, but the best friend is smarter than the dirtbag. They once recounted a masturbatory adventure using Tiger Balm as a lubricant. But, the best friend will go on to actually put his privilege and intellect to very good use in the world. More on him later.

In the beginning, before I could drive, I caught rides to and from band practice from the bass player. The interior of his Buick was covered in cigarette burns and had a rack of cassettes affixed to the bucket seat. But now I've got this van, a tank of a vehicle that requires either the foolishness of youth or the arm strength of a power lifter to steer. I guess you would call it a conversion as opposed to a passenger or cargo unit. It has captain's chairs rather than benches and a bed in the back. There is storage under the bed that would be perfect for human trafficking but bad for gear. Lately we've taken to storing all the instruments in between the captain's chairs and having everyone curl into the fetal position on top of the bed. We can fit the saxophone under the bed but that's about it.

Said van sits in the parking lot of my Catholic high school, a flower child relic surrounded by new German luxury sedans given as sweet sixteen presents to the privileged parasites in this algebra class. At this point my only friend in this whole building is the budding sociopath. He gives off what we would now call "Columbine vibes" and once called in a bomb scare so he could smoke in the parking lot while the school was evacuated. I'm realizing now that the one friend I had in high school might dislike being referred to as a budding sociopath. Let's call him Rambo from now on. He'll think that's funny, he's really into guns.

His dad is a Vietnam veteran with severe PTSD, though we don't know to call it that yet. Rambo sneaks up behind him and makes gunfire noises which cause the poor bastard to leap behind the couch in terror. Rambo appears to lack empathy and certainly has no love for our classmates. They are all terrified of him, which is great for me. In grade school I was mercilessly mocked to the point of wanting to harm myself. For better or worse, having this lunatic at my side keeps the proverbial wolves at bay.

He stashes a bottle of Jack Daniels in his locker and drinks several pots of coffee each day to balance himself out. He turns me on to Art Bell and we both get into Caspar Brötzmann. That is how we end up in a noise band together.

He built the telephone mic and finds quotes from old movies to play on a handheld cassette player run through eerie effects pedals. Sonically, it really ties the room together. He is also the band's media and brand manager. He writes manifestos and publishes hand-copied zines that are a blueprint for how to assemble a pistol and overthrow the government. Basically an eight-page domestic terrorist fantasy graphic novel. This is just that, fantasy. We are thrift store anarchists more interested in shock value than actual action. We are high and low minded. Our band name has a subtitle, "The Outbreak Of Theory," and a simple slogan, "Five Suits And A Telephone, Loud!"

At some point during our senior year, a local record store clerk and three other miscreants rent an empty building downtown. Kansas City has not yet gone through its coming gentrifying renaissance and downtown is still a shady character. A once vibrant cow town turned mafia haven is now a dark and dangerous distant memory of its former glory. Said miscreants build a stage and bring in a PA to turn this building into a venue.

Whether or not it is their intention from the start, the space can be open to all ages due to an inability to get a liquor license. It is haunted by all manner of disenfranchised teenagers, including myself, as well as a handful of ghosts. It is during the solitary year that this club is open that I learn more about the industry than I will ever learn in a class. How to run the door, how to sell merch, how to diffuse a fight and, most notably, how to perform on a stage.

If parents know where their children are, they are clutching their pearls in horror. The incredibly seedy gay gentlemen's tavern next door is allegedly the former hunting ground for a local serial killer. The dirtbag and his best friend, both hairless young boys, take payment from some old perverts there to touch the skin on their nubile teen stomachs. The only other bar on the corner may be patronized by actual pirates. It's the kind of place you go to find a man who knows how to dispose of a body. Within its smoked-stained walls you can find many of the bands on that night's bill pre-gaming before having to teetotal for teenagers in the club. It's where I would have been if I were in their shoes.

A Los Angeles-based pop anomaly is scheduled to perform at the club. He is the cousin of a local painter and performance artist who calls himself Skully because he had scoliosis as a child. Skully's cousin (who goes by the name Beck) has booked a series of all-ages spaces for his first tour. By the time he makes it to Kansas City his generation-defining first single has shot up the radio charts. Several thousand punkers descend upon our secret clubhouse. The local papers pick up the event, it is a cultural moment. Good for that month's rent, but it is the beginning of the end as more civilians are made aware of the place. Its very existence is, shall we say, not up to code, and in the coming months it will be gone, a hole in the ground soon to be surrounded by gastropub chains and white tablecloth BBQ joints.

Several other short-lived all-ages spots are started by my associates and others in the coming years. They all meet a similar fate. It's hard to make your nut if you can't sell booze to cover your overhead. Before the real estate boom some of the empty buildings in the area will rent out space for a night and let us put on shows. Soon local artists take advantage of the cheap rent on the wrong side of town and it all starts to change.

This is when I first learn the fundamental truth about any counterculture: there's a threshold of interested bodies that any strong underground can sustain before it gets corrupted. Whether that corruption is exploitation or destruction we all know that once something becomes too popular it ceases to be "cool" and it can never be the same again. The phoenix must be reborn from the ashes with the next generation, and the cycle repeats itself ad infinitum. This is the way.

Some enterprising young hood rats, friends with our drummer, start booking shows at a skate shop in the suburbs. The store is a mecca of decks, trucks and grip tape occupied by delinquents who fear neither injury nor death. Skaters, like nurses, are some of the wildest people in the world. They've seen so much pain inflicted on themselves or others that they are numb to it. It clouds their judgment and often leads to a reckless life. But I digress.

In the basement of the skate shop there is a large half pipe one must sign an insurance waiver in order to skate. We perch at the top, squeezing the usual diamond shape of our band's stage plot into an uncomfortable straight line. The crowd is in the bowl, and some thuggish hardcore kids have started steamrolling the pit. They line up at the back like they are playing red rover and run full force into the unsuspecting mob in the front. Those foolish enough to be watching the band are barreled over, their tender kneecaps colliding with the very hard wood of the ramp.

That's not the only problem. Some racist has shown up wearing a T-shirt featuring the image of a Klansman and the phrase "Boys in the Hood" written across the chest. This does not sit well with the SHARPs. The Skinheads Against Racial Prejudice, or SHARPs as they call themselves, are a skinhead sleeper cell from downtown. This crew is incredibly misogynistic and homophobic, but not racist. Traditional skinhead variations, at least around here, are more the militant white-nationalist type, but these are the good guys, I guess?

The SHARPs descend upon the bigot and proceed to beat him mercilessly, slamming his head against the metal staircase. This is our cue to leave. No doubt the authorities will be here soon and we don't need to be here to deal with them. This show is effectively over.

On the way home we ponder the nature of the motley crew that make up our scene. Punks, Grungies, Krishna straight-edgers, ska kids. The one thing that unites us is that we are all misfits, lurkers on the margins of polite society. We all go to different schools where at best we have one other friend who is "like us." The enemy of my enemy is my friend. The enemy, we think, is normalcy, the need to homogenize.

Our actual enemy, though we don't know it yet, is our own individual identities. All that we know is that we don't fit in with what our parents want us to be, so we try on different hats in an attempt to figure out who we really are. It's an exhausting process that must be exacerbated if you're having similar sexual or gender identity issues at this age. I can only imagine.

The E-word isn't being thrown around yet but it's not far off. The tribalism that will arrive with the coming technology will splinter this uneasy peace and make each niche much more insular. For the time being we are unified. It's all we can be, we literally only have each other.

In an effort to find more like-minded souls, I transfer to an art school. A shining beacon on the hill overlooking the wealthy white shopping district from the other side of the tracks. An inner-city experiment of magnets busing suburbanites into a brand spanking new prison complete with metal detectors and barred windows. It is either a glorious waste of taxpayer money or a symbol of enlightened celebration of the arts, depending on who you ask.

There is a quota that must be met in regards to the ethnicity of the students. In other words, this building is a powder keg of racial tension. It is not a fun place to be. Most days are spent skipping class to hide out in the black box theater or to leave campus entirely. We pass a smoke to the kindly old security guard and head to the diner down the road. That old geezer doesn't give a shit if we are in school.

At the diner we will order one bottomless cup of coffee for the entire table to share. We are still assholes. We will sit there and smoke and debate for the sake of debating. I won't tip because I am still a horrible person. Cup after cup, I am hooked on the black poison because of Honey White. When we met she partook, but I was innocent. I swallowed the sludge with fervor to impress her, presumably telegraphing that I was also a sophisticate. Now it has its hooks in me.

I am at this art school to learn writing, which I quickly realize can be taught anywhere. I'm not here for the many theaters or orchestras that are unique to this learning institution. I can learn to write English words well anywhere that it's spoken. So, in an act of desperation, I ask to be transferred back to the Jesuits. Honey White transfers, too, except she finds another school in the magnet experiment that emphasizes education.

It is still filled with the same tensions, but at least you need a 3.0 GPA to maintain enrollment. It's a much better flawed system.

I am aware that I come from means, though at this time I still think of myself as a victim. It will be years until I am able to process that my privilege put me ahead of the curve even if I dismissed it. I am a lawyer's son and my mother has remarried well. My brother and I, distant as always, live with them in an enormous house that is even larger than what we were used to. It has an intercom system for fuck's sake.

The kids in this Parish tend to skew wealthy. Catholic school isn't cheap after all, though it is a tax write-off for some ridiculous reason. One of my brother's associates is a piece of work. His father dropped dead of a massive heart attack while mowing the lawn when this kid was twelve. He hasn't seen much point in life, and therefore has become a burden on his widowed mother ever since.

He and my brother are smoking hash on the roof of our house after a rainstorm. A misstep on the wet shingles sends the friend careening off the ledge. He lands on the grass after first hitting the deck railing with his chest and the air conditioner with his ass. I see him fall past the living room window as I watch TV on the couch. We run outside and thankfully he's still breathing.

We will soon learn that he has broken ribs and a punctured lung. We are then informed that he is a runaway who has been hiding out at our house while our parents are on vacation. He refuses to call home or to go to the hospital since he is a minor and will be undoubtedly turned over to his mother. We finally convince him to call an uncle and he is out of our hair. It will be years until he's allowed at our house or near my brother again.

This may be the most clichéd thing I can say, but I do not get along with my stepdad. He's significantly older than my mom and very set in his ways. He hasn't had to deal with children, let alone teenagers, in a long, long time. He sits at the kitchen table eating tomato slices with cottage cheese and pepper. He drinks coffee and wears a bathrobe and nothing else. We've all seen his balls, even sleepover guests have gazed upon them. He is unashamed, it is his house after all.

He is thirty years sober and was apparently a really good time until he became a really mean drunk. A "close down the bar and then sleep in your car in the liquor store parking lot until it opens" sort of affair. It's through recovery that he met my mother. For some reason they still keep liquor in the house to entertain guests. I'll never understand that.

The house they bought has a full room-sized wine cellar that they have no use for. I convince them to turn the cave into a rehearsal room. They hire a contractor to soundproof the space, but he just puts up insulation which does next to nothing. You can still hear the drum kit throughout the whole house. This windowless dungeon soon becomes my primary residence in the house. I decorate the walls with graffiti, lyrics and fliers. Multicolored fairy lights and candles. It is a glorious escape from my real life.

Our Mutual Best Friend has been excommunicated from his mother's home so he has taken refuge on the mattresses here. He, too, has at one time seen my stepfather's balls, though neither that pendulously endowed old man nor my mother knows he's here right now. We wait until they go to work to emerge and partake of our pantry. At some point during this time, apropos of nothing, we steal a claw-foot bathtub. It's just a strange thing to steal. Soon he and I and Rambo will rent an apartment together and I will move out of the house the moment I am of age, before graduating and with no plan whatsoever. This will become a constant. The need to leave will be become a mantra for me, it will motivate everything that happens next.

My father moves to the East Coast. We don't really talk even when we do talk. It's not his fault, his dad doesn't talk either.

He watches the *Grand Ole Opry* and *Hee Haw* like the good ol' boy that he is. He takes me to an empty residential lot where he's cultivated what would now be called a "community garden." He is, in a word, handy. He can build things, fix most things, grow things, all that shit.

My grandfather used to pretend to forget my name but always asked me if I still played the "git-fiddle." He used to drive a city bus until a bout with mental illness landed him in an asylum. I won't learn about this particular family secret, that we are genetically predisposed to bipolar disorder, until well after I decide to bring my own children into the world. Would have been a good thing to be aware of. Just sayin'.

As age took its toll on my grandfather and he wasted away, my grandmother was by his side until the very end. It was an end that took too long to come and it exhausted her. For six glorious months after he passed she was the queen of the nursing home, barely having time in her schedule to see her visiting grandkids or new great-granddaughter. Then, half a year in to her freedom, she had a stroke that stole her everything. She could still walk, talk and eat, but had no idea what was going on or who any of us were. It was heartbreaking. It made me really dread the possibility of getting old.

My grandmother was a master seamstress, quilts being her chosen medium. She made elaborately patterned blankets as Christmas gifts for all her grandkids. On my wedding day she presented Honey White and me with a beautiful piece with the date stitched into the corner. She could do more with fabric than most painters can do with canvas and canned the most amazing sweet pickles, with green food coloring being the secret ingredient. It really gave them that lime Jell-O pop of color. Speaking of which, orange Jell-O with marshmallows and raisins anyone? Oh no, it's disgusting, but we ate it every Christmas.

In The Library

Our Mutual Best Friend, Rambo and I have moved into a rental house. It directly faces a busy thoroughfare and is next door to a liquor store that was once, as the story goes, my stepfather's camping spot. The house was converted into an office building before being rented to us and has carpet everywhere. Carpet in the kitchen, carpet in the bathroom, I'm surprised there isn't carpet on the porch.

The house has two bedrooms but we turn the dining room into a third with a series of curtains. It is an adult blanket fort. We agree to rotate who has to live in the fort every two months. We draw straws and Rambo takes the first shift. There is no privacy in the fort since it's the only access to both the kitchen and the bathroom. It is less than ideal.

The first week, Our Mutual Best Friend teaches us how to make potato soup. It's a very economical meal to make in large batches and keep in the fridge. It is merely a stick of butter, a bag of potatoes and a gallon of milk. Salt and pepper to taste. Some onions and garlic (any alliums really) as well as some thyme would go a long way, but what do I know. I guess it's beautiful in its simplicity but it's not fucking vichyssoise, I can tell you that much.

It takes about a week to finish off the soup between the three of us and another bag of potatoes is procured from the market. Since we are all weary of the dairy tuber broth we never make another batch. The spuds go into the pantry only to be found a year later when we move out. By then they had nearly decomposed completely and were most likely why we had so many mice even with the cat.

Monty, the black long hair, was a gift. Well, more precisely he was a friend's cat, and when that friend moved into a pet-unfriendly apartment he became ours. This is how I will acquire all pets for the foreseeable future. Even when Honey White and I start adopting dogs from the Humane Society. We only take animals that other people don't want or can't have.

Monty is from New Orleans, though at the time I don't know how cool that is. He came back with a bartender who acquired him on a road trip down south. He sat on her shoulder the whole thirteen-hour drive back to Kansas City. He is quite the mouser but cannot keep these creatures from the lure of a rancid sack of potatoes.

This winter, our heat goes out. Not because we didn't pay the bill, it's illegal to shut off the heat during a blizzard. The decades-old heater has given up the ghost. I sleep under seven blankets. Monty's water bowl freezes solid. I refuse to ask my parents for help. I got out of their place as soon as I was legal. I think of their house as a large, lavish prison free from need or worry. Foolishly, I live in squalor just to deny what I see as my oppression but will eventually realize is my privilege.

My roommates are disgusting. They don't clean, they don't do the dishes. They know that eventually I will do these chores because I have a controlling compulsion for order. As an experiment they leave a takeout soda in a wax-lined paper cup on a coffee table given to me by my parents that I assume is valueless but turns out to be an antique. The goal of the experiment is to see how long it takes either for the soda to dissolve the cup, or for me to clean up after them. I cave after three nights. The corrosive corn syrup-infused cocktail is now a house of flies and that is too much, even for me.

I work at the Linda Hall Library. It's a very fancy library. You can't even check out the books it's so exclusive. It's world renowned for science and locally renowned for a liberal hiring policy. I am a page, which means I fetch books and periodicals but soon will be promoted to the copy lab. If you want to leave the premises with the knowledge contained within these walls you'll have to take a Xerox.

We pages linger in the lounge playing computer solitaire and waiting for the pneumatic tubes to deliver our marching orders. We abscond with the request slip and wander off into the stacks to attempt to forage journals about biology or some such shit. The stacks are quiet and lonely. They would be a great place to have a salacious rendezvous if there was someone to have one with.

We are a motley crew at the Library. Some of us are "touched," as my grandmother used to say. Everyone here is at least slightly on the spectrum, some more than others. It seems to be a job free of consequence. Ghosting a page shift is perfectly acceptable. This place seems to draw people on the margins, and they apparently must be given a wide berth responsibility-wise. The couch in the break room is a coveted spot for rest. I've honed my nap skills and can manage to get an effective power slumber on my lunch break in as little as seven minutes.

When I'm promoted to the copy lab I am surrounded by the upper echelon of oddballs. My boss is a horror movie obsessive who writes Internet-based erotica as a side hustle. It's not hard, he says. The most difficult part is composing various euphemisms for penises. Once you get past the basic "manhood" or "member" or "muscle" you have to start thinking outside the box.

One of my fellow copy rats is a junkie. I don't know this yet, I think he's just tired all the time. He calls into work at 4:00 a.m. to announce his absence that day because he's gone "afoul of his bowels." Not a problem. As long as you call in before 8:00 a.m. you may be excused.

My coworkers are obsessed with an early Internet role-playing game that they play most of the day instead of working. I enter the break room to find my boss weeping into an ashtray because his character was killed in battle. Fuck, these people are weird, I love it. Gimme more, like the silent one who turns to face the wall when I pass him in the hallway, who eats his lunch out of a briefcase, yes please. I learn about so much new music, tape trading amongst all the staff is a common practice. It's a wonderful place to earn minimum wage.

My superior is a wise man but a coward. He fears change and despises when people leave his employ for personal growth. When I ask for three weeks off to go on my first touring adventure he informs me that it will fail. He is mistaken, of course. This will be the first of many musical traveling adventures I will partake in. I spend many of the next years determined to I prove him wrong.

Our Mutual Best Friend gets me a side gig at an adult video store. Besides renting exhausting amounts of pornography we also, apparently, deal drugs. My employers fail to mention the code name for an inhalant that is traditionally used as a tape-head cleaner. I am surprised when a customer asks for "Rush" and think he's talking about a concert film.

Everyone rents our films: local news celebrities, politicians, even the odd Catholic schoolteacher racking up stories to tell at confession. Humanity's appetite for pornography is impressive. Some particularly prolific marathon 'baters will leave with half a dozen blue boxes on a daily basis. It must take all the fun out of it, I think. It has to be more work than pleasure. More submitting to compulsion than enjoying the ecstasy of completion. I'm speculating, but this is maybe the most unique people-watching spot I've had before or since.

I am in school, but I am not in school. I receive a stipend from my father in order to pay for classes and cover some of my expenses. With the lump sum he sends at the beginning of the semester I purchase a 1972 extended body Ford Econoline

E250. You are right to sense a pattern, I will only purchase Econolines from this point forward. We Jam Econo, after all. I do not inform my father of this action. Instead I create a fake curriculum of classes, culminating in a notarized but completely counterfeit report card at the end of the semester. I learn this elaborate con from my older cousin, who also works at the Library. He actually pulled this off while living in his parents' house. My father lives thousands of miles away and is oblivious to my life, so the ruse is much easier for me.

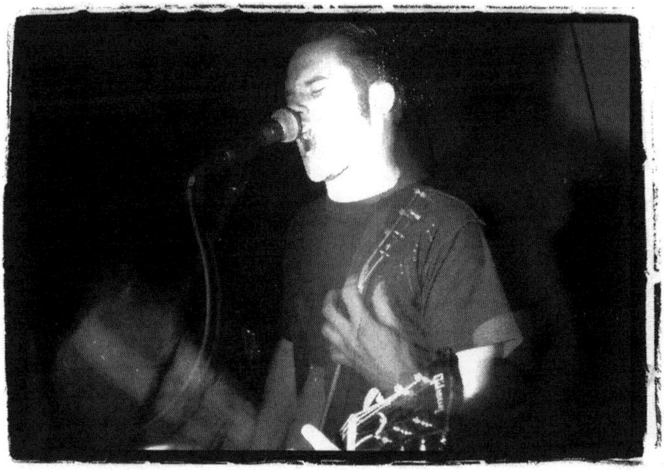

Suburban Get Up Kids

When my new band needs a name I veto the proposed original "suburban" prefix, ostensibly because of what I suspect is a letter-based curse. It's true that I'm coming off a solid two-year run of performing in local bands that all last mere months and all start with the letter "S," but the other reason is that I don't want to be associated with the suburbs. I'm from the city, or so I think.

I'm actually born of the original white-flight suburb that by this time has been absorbed by the greater Kansas City metropolitan area proper during expansion. However, I'm not going to get "Armour Hills" tattooed in old English across the top of my back. That's strictly for folks who come from the rough and tumble neighborhoods. I grew up going to a country club, but at least I'm not from Johnson County.

I met Jim and The Popes when their high school band played shows with several of my high school bands. They are from the suburbs and don't seem bothered by that pedigree. They come to our club house in the city. They like abstract feedback-based noise rock even more than me. They all wear glasses and are much more fashionable than me and my mechanic chic. Jim and I are in one of the doomed "S" bands for a while. He fights with the bass player, who is older and set in his ways. He's an opinionated pain in the ass but his ideas are really good. So, when it comes time to choose sides, I stick with Jim.

We want to do something different. Something we can't quite explain, something we think we've seen people come close to doing, but not quite. We recruit Rob and start playing with a drummer who is a sculptor named Nathan that Jim knows from art school. Nathan is a straight edge hardcore type and he introduces us to both Lifetime and Avail. He proclaims that it's better to see a bad band play with energy than a great band just stand on stage like a tree stump. I don't think we necessarily agree but it's an interesting philosophy.

We try to become a great band that plays with energy. A pop group that isn't afraid of onstage chaos. We write songs that allow for movement and are filled with teenage angst and the anxiety of our lives. We are also discovering, though we don't know it yet, that this strange cocktail is only achievable through sincerity. We actually have to believe in what we're doing, we have to actually love the songs that we're singing and embrace every place that we play them. We write by three basic but unspoken edicts: the quiet-loud, the octave fog, and that half time is the right time. This will suit us well in the coming years.

Meanwhile, Rambo is in a band with Ryan and is learning how to play guitar, sort of. He's taken the precision stringed instrument capable of creating tear-inducing melodies and turned it into a medieval torture device. He uses distortion and delay in combination with feedback to create terrifying, punishing soundscapes. This seems to be the point. He revels in testing the limit of what music can, or some might say *shouldn't,* achieve. It is unique, but I have to wonder if it's more fun to create and perform than it is to actually listen to. Maybe that's just me.

He has teamed up with a drummer who everyone refers to as "Pat The Head," whose Charlie Brown-like dome is his most distinguishing feature. It's not meant as an insult, he introduces himself as such. Rambo's new outfit rehearses and sometimes performs in Pat The Head's basement. It's an even dingier house than ours, in a tense neighborhood where weapons and street drugs are not uncommon. For a few months, Pat The Head's house becomes the place to see or be seen in Kansas City. It's close to the art school and therefore the scene is a mix of trust-fund Picassos and bitter blue-collar street toughs. Skate rats drink Mickey's wide mouth bullets and Old English 40s on the lawn. It's pretty much a sausage party save for the few femmes tough or crazy enough to put up with their bullshit.

Regional and national bands start coming to Pat The Head's basement, most likely self-routed using *Book Your Own Fuckin' Life*. Two NYC bands called Shift and Texas Is The Reason are supposed to play. Seems both of their vans have had technical issues and they have to cancel last minute. This is, I assume, utter horseshit. Reasonable but untrue. I know I wouldn't be excited to get a tour itinerary with a door deal at "Pat The Head's Basement." In any case our new band, if you can even call it that yet, are all in attendance. Rambo's new band are already on the bill. If we can use their gear we can play a couple of these new songs we've been writing. So, unceremoniously, and probably with a speed similar to that of someone losing their virginity, we play our first show. It is uneventful in the minds of all in attendance, but an addictive thrill for the four of us.

Over the coming months we continue to write. Jim has started working at the Library. We trade cassettes and wander the stacks wearing headphones, oblivious to the world outside this nuclear bunker filled with scientific tomes. A plan is hatched. It is a noble if simplistic plan. We will record a single and use that as a catalyst to go on tour, maybe find a record label.

There is a recording studio in Nebraska that charges by the song rather than by the hour. This is not a very profitable business model on their part but it is a way to gain experience as an engineer or producer. We pack up the '78 Econoline and make our way north. As we roll into town the engine seizes shut and we are no longer running on just fumes, we are running on nothing. We roll down a hill in neutral and miraculously coast into a petrol station.

We record three songs and the Sculptor insists that he scream on each one. We're not crazy about this, but he seems adamant so we let it go. It's not really the sound we're going for and I have no fucking idea what he's saying in any of these songs. He certainly hasn't consulted with me about what the lyrics are about, if not literally then at least metaphorically. I don't know if we're contradicting each other in the same song. It's schizophrenic, or maybe schizo-phonic is more accurate.

We are happy with two of the three, "Shorty" and "The Breathing Method," and decide to release them on vinyl. A pressing is ordered, as well as poly bags to put them in. We take individual photobooth photos at our favorite diner and use flier-making technology to construct the covers and inserts. My photo lab skills have been well honed, and I basically print the whole thing for free when my coworkers are in the break room. It was cheaper to press the vinyl with blank labels so we have a stamp made at the local office supply store and spend the next few nights stamping and assembling the singles. It is a modest affair. On the second pressing a friend who actually knows graphic design will clean up the lines in the art, but this first pressing is, well, rustic.

We mail the disc to every address we can find. Some friends from the Library play in a band that has actually toured so they give us some contacts. There is the aforementioned *Book Your Own Fuckin' Life* bible as well as the label P.O. boxes on the back of our favorite records. Surprisingly, there is some interest. We start to set up our own shows out of town, usually in a basement or a VFW hall within a four-to-eight-hour driving radius, but it's looking more and more like we might be able to actually book a tour over the coming summer.

The Sculptor has been offered an internship over the summer break and chooses that path over the possibility of touring. The tour is just hypothetical at this point, but this conflict obviously won't work, so we inform him that if he doesn't want to do the tour we will look for a drummer who will. He doesn't take it well. He throws such a spectacular tantrum that it's embarrassing to even recount it. He grabs a copy of the vinyl we've just self-released and breaks it in half to symbolize the breaking of our friendship. Very dramatic. If I'm being honest it wasn't a good match anyway. This is for the best, we tell ourselves.

As a purely temporary measure we enlist Ryan on the drums. Jim is especially hesitant about this. Those two push each others' buttons. Plus, Ryan is still in high school, too young to tour. But it soon becomes obvious that he is the right man for the job and so he is made a permanent addition. We're just gonna have to work around the age thing. Luckily the younger brother is already adept at keeping secrets. What his folks don't know won't hurt them.

The tour takes us to places like Way Cool Records in Chicago, Amanda's basement in St. Louis, Clunk Records in Fayetteville, Arkansas, and a place called Sparks in Louisville, Kentucky, where there are larger than life black and white photos of incredibly fit men in their underwear all over the dance floor. The Slant House in Madison, Wisconsin, is where we are set to play with an Austin band called Mineral and a Milwaukee band called the Promise Ring.

This is the gig of legend, but it isn't that great or well attended. We load our gear down the skinniest and creakiest flight of stairs imaginable and set up on the floor. When it's our time to play we make quite the ruckus and the people watching us pound their chests in rhythm, adjusting their glasses and seemingly empty backpacks. Later, I catch the Promise Ring playing a mix tape on their van's stereo. I am surprised by their un-ironic love for Top 40 pop radio and the hits of today. It leaves an impression on me. Maybe bands on the radio are cool? I've been so steeped in the indie rock underground and noise scene that I forgot what a joy pop music is.

Next there's Bug's House in Cedar Falls, Iowa. We are in the middle of nowhere on Friday the 13th. There is a scattering of teens and twentysomethings on the lawn, many of them drinking, some tripping on LSD. This is a different sort of crowd, a mix of punks, rednecks, nerds and jocks, a real "Breakfast Club" of humanity. It's not the homogeny of glasses, backpacks and white belts we are familiar with. This is a small town, you've got to make your own fun.

I learn that this isn't actually Bug's house, it's his mom's place and Bug doesn't live here anymore. I prep a Cup O' Noodles in the kitchen and a sandpaper voice ravaged by decades of smoking beckons behind me. "That smells good, wish I could have some." I turn to tell the voice that I've got another cup if they want it but find myself looking at an older woman with a feeding tube in her stomach. She reaches into a drawer to withdraw a hypodermic syringe and fills it with Peppermint Schnapps. After mainlining the shot into her tube she gives me a "Thanks, Darlin'" and retires to the living room. Her and her "Old Man" are watching *The Empire Strikes Back*, and next to her BarcaLounger he's got an IV drip bag full of what appears to be beer. This must be Bug's mom, I tell myself, I see why he doesn't want to live here.

The show is weird. A hippie girl who's tripping balls tells us she can see our aura. A stoner says we sound just like The Jesus Lizard. We don't sound anything like The Jesus Lizard. Our handsome Mormon merch guy convinces many of the patrons that our vinyl 7" is actually an oversized CD. Surprisingly, this works more times than you would think. We actually have a decent merch haul at this shit show. The Popes procure us a place to stay and I fall asleep listening to our two female hosts attempting to explain the values of the band Phish.

Most of the shows in Kansas City are either at a coffee shop in the 'burbs or at the VFW Hall in midtown. I've started booking shows at the hall with Rambo's help. To secure the space it's a hundred-dollar deposit that must be hand-delivered in cash to an old veteran's apartment. His place reeks of cigarettes and whiskey, and he's got a impressive amount of collectible commemorative plates. One corner of his display is dedicated to the British royal family, with Princess Diana staring out from the center not long before her death. Just pay the man and let's get the fuck out of here.

Show day at the VFW Hall is eclectic. There is one Lookout Records-style punk band and one Epitaph Records-style punk band. This distinction is very important, these are warring factions. The rise of popular punk's presence on the radio has been divisive. There's a lot of talk about what's "real" and what's "sellout." Gilman Street and Reverend Norb are brought up a lot. Absolute devotion to The Ramones as "The Greatest Punk Band Of All Time" is mandatory. I'm kinda more into The Clash, but whatever.

There is also a ska band made up of three brothers. They are unabashedly from the suburbs and wear the Joco label proudly. They're gonna sign a big label deal soon, as is the Epitaph-style punk band. This is rare for outfits from this area. Rounding out the bill is a hardcore band and us, labeled with the dreaded E-word years before it was cool. The hardcore band, Coalesce, is already being considered groundbreaking in that scene. They are fun as hell to watch, but I have no idea what the fuck is going on. As a reformed noise rocker myself I assume that's all this is, but apparently there is a lot more happening than my simple mind can comprehend.

The singer of the Lookout-style punk band is drinking in the parking lot and starting to get mouthy. His bandmates are both teetotalers and are getting sick of his shit. The band is on the brink of collapse every show, but fuck me if their songs aren't great. I don't know it yet but a lot of the components of what will come to be known as "our scene" are already present. Some of these people will start bands that we will take under our wing and take on the road. They are a few years from being fully formed but we're already set in stone. If only we weren't a "fucking emo band" all would be right with the world.

Close To Home

As a glorified book gopher I meet all manner of musical misfits who work at the Library. There's a country artist who is the best guitar player in town, both the guitar player and the bass player in Boys Life, my favorite local band, and a couple members of Acronym Girl's favorite, Mongol Beach Party. We are equals in the eyes of our employer, but around these guys I'm still the obsessive kid absorbing any information that comes my way.

I've been fascinated with Boys Life since I was in high school. I somehow convinced these cool kids in workmen's coats to do a split 7" that I self-released with my noise rock outfit. I couldn't believe it when they agreed to the release, but I guess everyone is desperate to put music out. They play a style somewhere in between punk and indie rock and will come to be called the E-word just like me, but nobody says that yet. Their first drummer was a maniac. I found him huffing paint after one of their shows and I later heard that's the night they literally kicked him out of the van and the band for good. He was a beast on the kit though. Their new drummer is a cat I've known for years, even played with him for a minute. When he got the call I encouraged him to take it, much to the disappointment of our bandmates. Why would you keep playing with us when you could be in the best band in town?

I follow the guitar player of Boys Life around like a puppy. He's only a couple years older than me but has been on tour several times. Before my band gains notoriety they will be the reference point for our city to the rest of the musical underground around the country. He gives me phone numbers of promoters and advice on how to build a loft in the van. They are all ex-skaters and have experience building ramps so a bunk bed is rudimentary carpentry for them. I've never built a birdhouse so it's all new to me.

One of the contacts is a guy with a funny name in Boston who knows a girl that Honey White will go to college with. Small world, I think to myself, but it might be a way to get him to book us. It's Boys Life's name that I will throw around in the coming months to let potential promoters know that we are serious, a band worth taking note of. If this band vouches for us then you know we're solid, at least that's what I tell myself. Truth is, it's probably the popularity of our first self-released record that perks people's ears up.

Boys Life eventually changes their sound. They take what I can only describe as a more "mature" approach to songwriting. I like it, but not as much as the old stuff. I'm not "that guy" who only likes their first record, I respect their choice to evolve, but it doesn't move me in the same way. I will myself into obsessing over the record anyway, so much so that we will go on to make our first album with the same producer.

I do take note of how they've abandoned their previous work, refusing to play most, if any, of the songs from the first release. This is off-putting to the crowd and I drink that in. I know that you have to make creative decisions for yourself, but disowning the songs that gained you fans in the first place seems to be ill-advised in my observation. The bass player says they can't play the old songs because they wouldn't be "sonic-ly correct." Even at this impressionable young age I call bullshit on that.

They change their amps, too, moving from half-stacks to combos. The guitarist I follow around used to be able to do that Drive Like Jehu thing where you make fluttering guitar feedback, like the call of some weird distorted bird. It's some perfect alchemy of a specific guitar, amp and speaker cabinet. It's a really unique sound that I've never been able to replicate even after I buy his amp. He starts playing through a Fender

Twin which does look cool but wouldn't distort unless you cut the speaker cones in half.

Here's the other thing about my favorite local band: those motherfuckers cannot stand each other. They are all bullish and obstinate alphas and will eventually come to blows. That this is exactly how the dynamic in my own band will become is not lost on me today. This is the way I was taught.

Boys Life are on tour when their van catches fire. That bitchin' Dodge with the extended ceiling was the envy of the entire Kansas City music scene. Apparently while they were sleeping off the dawn at a truck stop something caught flame and soon the entire vehicle was engulfed. Everyone escaped and the gear was saved but the van was lost. They rented a box truck and drove home to receive a hero's welcome at our local haunt. They played their songs like one can only after a near death experience and it was the greatest show I've ever seen.

That is the end for them. I imagine coming that close to death would put things in perspective and maybe convince one that touring isn't the most stable of professions. Some of them start other bands and eventually move to DC. I wouldn't be where I am if it weren't for them and I am grateful to have learned from their mistakes and successes. I can't say I always followed their example, nor did I avoid it, but it cannot be overstated how big a part of me that band is.

My favorite local band aside, the two very best bands in the entire fucking world are from Lawrence, Kansas. Kill Creek is a rock band that probably got labeled "alternative" in their day but would have been squarely in the E-word category now, and the other is an indie pop trio called Vitreous Humor. I'm not really familiar with this college hamlet they call Moscow On The Kaw. The first time I ever came to Lawrence was when I was fifteen and had to wait outside a club in South Park until it was time to perform. Club 21 was the name of the venue. In later years the building would house my acupuncturist and then a cigar shop.

There is a disconnect between Lawrence and Kansas City that I think I understand at first, but will understand less once I later move here. There is a reason that the two very best bands come from this town. I've never been able to put my finger on what the vibrancy of this place is, but it's palpable. Maybe it's the influx of new students every year at the university, a cultural blood transfusion of creative young people to revitalize the town.

Back to Kansas City, we need to sidebar a minute to talk about Quitters Club. First off, best band name ever. Secondly, I don't think I've ever seen another band, outside of Shellac or NOFX, that gave less of a fuck about the crowd. The first time I saw them was in a basement, and the singer accidentally punched himself in the mouth with the microphone and proceeded to bleed all over his shirt as well as everyone else in that basement for the rest of their set. At a record store show they played nothing but feedback for thirty minutes until the entire room cleared. It wasn't until the venue was empty that they started playing an actual song. Their songs were angular and weird and loud and angry and the best thing ever. End of lecture.

There is a thing called the Kansas City Music Scene but we are not a part of it. None of the aforementioned bands are. Our own scene is disparate and disjointed. When we start to travel we learn about communities that support their bands and it's a somewhat foreign concept. Louisville is the first place where we learn a band's biggest market should be their hometown. Local kids made good. We don't have that, we'll have to escape this place in order to find our fortune. I, for one, cannot wait to leave.

Most of the venues in this town are 21+ which means I can't be in the audience but I can still perform there. The first time I played Davey's Uptown was when I was sixteen. Ernie from Sin City Disciples took a shine to Secular Theme and invited us to open for his new project. I waited outside next to a sex toy shop called Ray's Playpen until it was my time to take the stage. In my black suit and skinny tie I made quite a racket with my thrift store guitar and Peavey 4×10 combo amplifier. Afterwards, the big man himself invited us back to his place to "smoke a joint a see Jah," but I politely declined. It wasn't really my scene.

Davey's Uptown is not to be confused with Dave's Stagecoach. The former is a dive bar of the highest caliber. If it hadn't burned to the ground I would perform there any day of the week. The latter is a lifer bar, not a venue, but it is across the street from the Hurricane. We call it "the Herpes-cocaine" since that's the scene at that club. The bartenders are all attractive women with full sleeves rendered by either Whispering Danny or Bill The Drill (so named for his liberal use of pressure on those in his chair), the two tattoo legends in town. The Hurricane sucks. We played there only once and the owner tried to stiff us. That pretty much sums the place up.

As far as all-ages shows there are a couple of options besides random abandoned warehouses, art spaces or basements. The Daily Grind is a coffee shop across the street from Whispering Danny's place, Exile Tattoo (it's called Exile because it's on Main Street, figure it out). The Daily Grind is small and I don't think I've even had coffee there, but the gigs are cool. My pop punk outfit performed there in the early days. I saw Kevin Seconds pass out on that same stage.

I watched Propagandhi back when John K. Samson was still in the band, and it was the most disgusting smell I've ever encountered. Two hundred gutter punks who hadn't bathed in weeks gathered together in one room. It makes me want to vomit just thinking about it. I didn't go see Cap n' Jazz there even though I wanted to. They broke up the next day. Fuck.

One time we went to a mixed bill of noise rock and ska. We were there to see the noise duo godheadSilo. When we arrived there was a massive tour bus parked in front of our tiny haunt. No Doubt, months before they broke big, were sandwiched into this show because they had a day off from their tour opening for Bush. They performed with all the pomposity of proper rock stars, which was out of place for this venue. They clashed with the other bands. One of them asked a member of godheadSilo for a light and knocked the dart out of their hands. It was poor form on their part and it became a touchstone for me. Bad gigs come and poorly attended shows are inevitable, even at the height of your popularity, but how are you gonna choose to handle it? I choose to narrow my focus and give everything for the people that are here. Others decide to throw a temper tantrum. I don't want to be someone like that.

We played a gig at The Daily Grind on the night of Jim and The Popes' high school prom. They took their dates out to dinner in a limo, popped into the gig and performed in their ill-fitting tuxedos, and then fucked off to the dance. I took care of load out. At this gig I sang into my new favorite microphone, which I called a "potato mic" because of its shape. It's the kind of microphone you've seen Elvis use, one you can cup in your hand. It sounded like shit but it looked cool as hell, like something John Reis would use.

I don't know if enough people acknowledge it, but Reis was the gold standard for style at the time. His slicked-back hair, gold top Les Paul and Hawaiian or Western shirts were the height of fashion for me. We adapted a look loosely based on his San Diego chic but with a mechanic and janitor uniform flair. The guitar player from Boys Life told me about a place called Uniform Supply located in a scary neighborhood past downtown. I bought slacks and a workman's jacket. I looked more ready to fix your transmission than sing you a song.

For other all-ages adventures you had to go to the suburbs and hit up Gee Coffee, which seemed like it must have been a front for something. Their second location was massive and had a PA that would be appropriate for an amphitheater. We came here and did what teenagers always do, linger. Looking back, it's interesting that I never actually drank coffee at any of these places.

Jim and The Popes are from this part of town and so many of their high school friends attend when we play. As previously mentioned, I don't like the suburbs. Even though I come from money, I desperately want to be blue collar. I dress like a grease monkey and carry myself with a "put your head down and get the work done" ethic. My privilege is shameful to me, I don't really like the other kids in our tax bracket.

I am a lawyer's son. I am proud of my father for representing labor though I would never tell him that. His own father was a bus driver and he wanted to take care of people like him. He used his large intellect to represent teachers, firefighters, flight attendants and eventually professional athletes. There are photos of me with an anti-TWA shirt when I was just a few years old during the strike that Reagan broke. I found myself actually defending the baseball players' strike in the '90s to my high school classmates because my father, who was striking with them, explained that the owners were fucking over the players and they just wanted their fair share. I didn't care about baseball or any of those assholes at school but this principle was important and I felt a need to defend it.

We don't really have a gigger's union. The transient and isolationist attitudes of touring musicians don't seem to lend themselves to organized labor. Plus, everyone thinks we're spoiled brats anyway because we kind of act like it. Extended adolescence and all, it's really one of the only jobs where you're encouraged to drink and do drugs at work. I struggle with this when people start to call me an artist.

I'm not comfortable with that word and I don't really even like calling myself a musician. Artists paint and musicians can sight read sheet music and know music theory. I'm in a band that plays shows, that's it. As I get older I will start to become resentful that our field doesn't get more respect in the traditional "arts" sense. There are no artist-in-residence grants for rock and roll singers, but then again nobody screams along to the title of a painting.

Eventually Jacki Becker takes notice of us. She works at The Bottleneck in Lawrence and is starting to book some shows there. The Bottleneck is the foundation of the Lawrence music scene. If The Outhouse is the CBGB's of the Midwest, The Bottleneck is maybe The Troubadour. Oh shit, have we not talked about The Outhouse? Four miles east of Lawrence there is a square cinder block building in the middle of a corn field. This is The Outhouse. I don't know how it got started, but sometime back in the day they started having punk shows here.

Everyone played The Outhouse on their first tour, at least everyone but me. I never got to perform at this legendary club. I did, however, have an interesting experience when Honey White and I had our mutual bachelor / bachelorette party there, after it had become a BYOB strip club. She bought me an onstage lap dance where the lovely ladies took off my studded heavy metal belt and whipped me with it. I had welts on my legs while reciting our wedding vows the next day.

Anyway, playing The Bottleneck was a big deal, especially to a bunch of teenagers. JB put us on a Monday night bill opening for a band called Speed McQueen, hoping that our younger fanbase would come out in force to pad the show. Our younger fanbase didn't live in Lawrence and couldn't have come to this 21+ show anyway so the whole thing was a bust. There were more people onstage than in the crowd.

JB takes care of us, though. Her career will run parallel to ours. She'll be the one to tell us we can't play on New Year's Eve because the band drinks more than the crowd does. She'll limit our alcohol intake at shows to make sure we don't make fools of ourselves. She is our biggest advocate and she suffers us with grace.

Lawrence is also home to The Replay Lounge, a pinball-themed dive bar that, according to legend, sells more PBR than any other place in Kansas. This will become my local after I move to this fair city. We once watched the Promise Ring and Jets To Brazil play during a hundred-year flood that would have claimed some of the gear in our basement if we hadn't hurried home to rescue it. I saw Modest Mouse there and they were wretched. An introspective indie rock nerd I worked with saw a timid man named Elliott Smith whisper his songs there over a barely perceptible crowd. We only played the Replay once back in the day, opening for Chavez.

For now I'm still in Kansas City, where I get a new job at Recycled Sounds. The record store is a safe haven for musically minded misfits and I get to sell them records. Really though, I organize cassettes and posters but I'm still excited to work here. There's a space in the back of the store where bands can set up and play. Man or Astro-man?, the Delta '72, and all the Caulfield Records bands from Omaha come and perform. When it's our turn to play there our friend The Photographer gets some sweet shots of the show. Afterward we go to our favorite buffet, China Tom's, and take a photo in the mirrored bathroom. Surely that didn't look suspicious, an older man and four young boys heading into the men's room of a Chinese restaurant. Perfectly wholesome.

Besides these venues you really have to make your own luck. There's the VFW Hall which is hit or miss, those random warehouses and art galleries, maybe The Head's place or some other basement, but we don't really have a club to call home. I'm proud of being from here but I'm not sure if it's reciprocated. They make it hard to be a band in this town. It's Boys Life that cracked the code. The only way to succeed here is to leave and come back as conquerors.

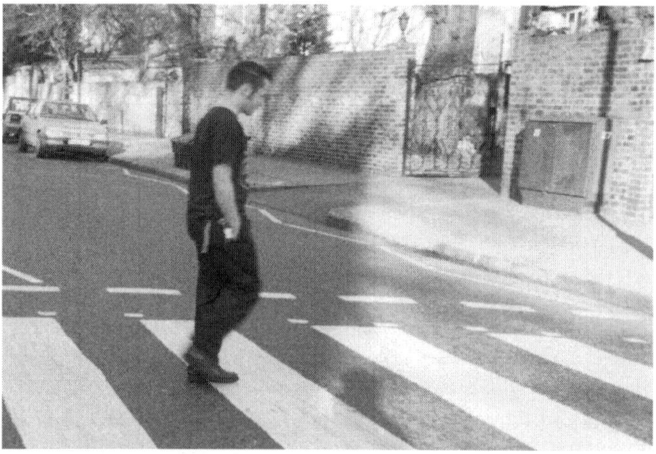

Better Half

I am kneeling over the toilet in the second story bathroom of my future in-laws' house vomiting uncontrollably. I will come to know these as panic attacks but at this time I assume it's from the wine. I've had a whole two glasses of merlot in the hopes of calming my nerves but no such luck. In between heaves I steady myself over the bowl and attempt to slow my breathing. I don't want to pass out. I lie down on the cold floor and wait for the distress to pass.

It's the night before Honey White is going to make the fourteen-hundred-mile drive to Boston with her parents and kid sister. Even codependent me is self-aware enough to know that offering to move there with her would be a bad look, not that she asked anyway. She's off to university, a small liberal arts school exclusively for women. They gave her a hefty sum to attend, and besides, this has always been her dream. Well, the first part of her dream anyway. She also wants to get her PhD, but that's still a ways off. Tomorrow is the first day of the rest of her life.

I can't help but feel that her decision to move halfway across the country is somewhat about me. I shamefully feel abandoned and scared, too selfish to even entertain the notion that this might be part of the reason she wants to put distance between us. There was another smaller but still excellent school that was only two hours from Kansas City, but I think she knew that she would never have her own life independent of me being that close. I can't read her thoughts, but she tells me that she's doing this exclusively for her. It's a fantastic opportunity after all. I am aware of this but it's still difficult to accept that she's leaving.

The next night, Our Mutual Best Friend teaches me how to drink tequila at the enormous apartment we share in a bad part of town. He buys a bottle of sorority girl Reposado and pours each of us a shot. I down the cheap brown liquor and wince as it burns its way down the back of my throat. Monty the cat stares on judgmentally. He knows where this is going.

Our Mutual Best Friend and I talk about Honey White's departure. He's blue about it as well. She's been both the source of our initial rivalry and ultimately what bonded our friendship. We both love her, I'm just *in love with* her and now she's gone away. He pours another shot and proposes a toast to her. The second shot is for friends we've lost.

Monty leaps suddenly to the height of the vaulted ceiling to catch a cicada. It scares the ever-living shit out of us. Third shot goes on the floor, he proclaims, as he dumps both jiggers over the hard wood. We should probably mop that up, we're gonna get ants. Fourth shot is a toast to Monty, slayer of insects, feline king of Kansas City, ruler of his domain, master of all. Fifth shot is to...I don't remember. I don't remember anything after that.

I awake in bed the next morning still in my jeans and mechanic's jacket. My head surprisingly isn't pounding, which is a relief. Maybe I took some ibuprofen and water before I passed out? I drink coffee quickly and then drive myself to class. I'm attending community college after flunking out of the local state university. I've decided to study business because I want to be a musician and this is the only thing that seems to be anywhere near that wheelhouse. My logic is that it is the music *business*, so how different could it be? What I haven't discovered yet is that these classes basically teach you how to be an accountant.

I slide into my desk and the room gets blurry. Oh fuck, I'm still drunk. *Ok, ok, keep it cool, you shouldn't drive home but it's too* far to walk. Ok, ok, just drive real, real slow and be extra aware of the road. I white knuckle it all the way back to the apartment and go back to sleep.

Honey White and I talk every day. We were on-again, off-again for a couple of years through high school, but since we're currently on-again we're gonna try and make it work long distance. Thus the daily phone calls. She tells me about the sprawl of the city and strange and interesting people she's met, many of them lesbians. One such specimen has taught her how to breathe fire. Great, I say, secretly wondering if she really wants to run off and join the circus.

Her roommate in the dorms seems normal enough, but we will soon realize that she is, in fact, unhinged. She thinks Honey White is from the middle of nowhere even though this roommate is from a tiny cranberry town off the cape. There's more people in Kansas City than where she's from, but that's how Massholes are. They never seem to understand why anyone wouldn't want to live near "Bahstan."

I tell Honey White the band is picking up steam. We've already recorded three songs, released our own 7", and gotten a rejection letter from Warner Bros. My presence looms over her as the band's popularity grows and I write more and more songs about her specifically and New England in general. It seems to be off-putting to her. This is supposed to be a respite for her yet many of her peers are infatuated with her boyfriend's band back home.

I come to visit in the winter during nor'easter season. She slips on the icy sidewalk and I catch her before she falls as we walk to her dorm. It's against school policy to have men sleep over so I have to hide, but her roommate doesn't care and the other students couldn't give any less of a shit either, as they have suitors of all genders stay the night all the time. Besides avoiding the RA the only real trick is using the toilet. I send Honey White in ahead to make sure the coast is clear and she stays on lookout until I have either done my business or taken the world's fastest shower. Sex is an awkward and silent affair in a twin bed, not wanting to wake the lunatic snoring mere steps away from us.

Honey White takes me to her favorite record store, her favorite place to see shows, and her favorite bar. We're both underage but can get pints at any number of taverns that turn a blind eye to the students. They'd all go belly up if they carded every one of the teens in a town filled with universities. We go to her favorite diner late at night after shows like we did back home. It's really the same routine just in a bigger city, meaning better food and more frequent events. She seems happy. I assume it's because I'm here, but it might really be in spite of that. She loves me but I am a lot, especially now that my music has infiltrated her world away from me. She loves school, loves the act of learning, loves being in the city. I smile and try to meet her enthusiasm but I really wish she would just come home.

The distance between us is motivating. I write lyrics about her, naming the songs after the city, state, and routing of our upcoming tours. The very first time we play Boston it is because of the contact with a funny name that I got from Boys Life. The show takes place in a house on Mission Hill, on a block I have already walked several times. It was kind of a shit show. I could not hear the vocals through the weak PA at all and sang on faith. We plowed through our set surrounded by white-belted hipsters.

After the show, I sneak back to the dorms while the rest of the boys find a trust fund kid's house to sleep at. The next morning I linger, even though she has to go to class. We only have a two-hour drive so, thankfully, I can make time to walk her to school. She reluctantly agrees, she's ready to get back to her life. Inside of this university during her day-to-day life I am inconsequential, but at our show it has everything to do with me. She's not crazy about that particular baggage especially when people in the scene come to think of her as "my girlfriend" as opposed to a strong and independent woman in her own right.

I don't fully grasp the concept at this age, but the misogyny in this scene is ever present, especially on the East Coast. Hardcore seems to be mostly a male-dominated medium. It makes sense—it's aggressive, angry and sometimes violent. This fucking emo trash is more introspective and sensitive even though it can be just as loud and bombastic. It will lead the singer of one world-renowned and particularly intense New York hardcore outfit to declare: "I like these emo shows, there's lots of chicks here."

However, even in our little scene there aren't many females on stage, there aren't many people of color onstage, and there certainly aren't any openly queer folks at the mic either. It's a very, very white male scene, at least as far as the bands go. The crowd is actually pretty gender diverse and the femmes are probably the driving force behind the genre's popularity. Not "probably," I *know* they are.

Honey White has already been telling me this for years, even before I started touring. The Kansas City scene was the pits for her, filled with sexist skaters and punks who never took her seriously. I couldn't see it, or, really, I didn't want to admit it. Punk rock saved my life and I couldn't bear the idea that it could be hurting someone that I cared so much about. I was in denial, not just a river in Egypt, that evil specter I had learned to fear so much in the support group. But this wasn't making excuses for an addict's behavior, this was putting on blinders to the actions of people you care about. At the time, I really thought that being a one-woman man was enough. I know now that my silence and inaction was part of the problem. You don't fix anything by not speaking up.

The struggle for me is that I can't see my privilege, not yet anyway. We're years away from calling it that, but that's what it is. In my mind, I was a misfit, an outsider. I was bullied and harassed and now I've found a group of people who not only are like me but want to hear the music I make. Music that is about feeling awkward and lonely and frustrated. It's hard for me to wrap my young brain around any other narrative except that I've been the victim. I know now that this is absurd, but I was young and really thought I had it hard.

When the Riot Grrrl movement started I didn't get it. I understood women feeling oppressed in regular society, but we're all in the same boat here, right? We're all misfits and part of the same counterculture, but that sexism still existed inside of our scene. There is a big uproar at a Bikini Kill show at the VFW Hall. The singer in one of the opening bands is a skater who has a very public reputation for being a womanizer. Someone even put up fliers around town advertising him as having stolen her record collection. His band should not be opening this show.

Back in Boston it's particularly bad. The hardcore kids have now started playing more, for lack of a better word, "emotional" music. Other than one drummer who Honey White and I have befriended, everyone else seems to be a meathead. Maybe it's just me, but the hardcore guys remind me of the football players that used to harass me in high school. I never quite gel with them, even when we play shows together. Even weirder, when one of these bros tells me that he works out to our music I have nothing to say. I don't relate to this person at all. I'm an awkward greaser with abandonment issues who is unhealthily obsessed with a wicked smart girl, surely I don't write songs that you can lift weights to, right?

In The Doghouse

We've sent our self-released 7" to every record label address we could find. We've received rejection letters and general disinterest from all parties except for two. The first is a one man, kitchen table sort of affair. The kind of project one takes on in their college years. To call it a label would be generous.

The other is an established indie label in the hardcore scene. The hardcore scene is, if we're being honest, not for us. The heavy music that I grew up on was more experimental in nature, more motivated by noise than anger. It's only Jim's deep love of Helmet than even remotely tethers us to NYHC. We only find out after the fact that our friends and partners in crime at Initial Records in Louisville, Kentucky, had wanted to work with us but didn't ask out of professional courtesy. Fuck me if things wouldn't have worked out differently if they had.

Desperation is a motivating thing, and our desire to release the four songs that we've recently recorded and paid for out of pocket leads to a phone call with The D Man. The D Man's label is based out of Toledo. I've never been to Ohio but will soon learn that it's an odd duck of a state. The fact that it seems to decide every presidential election is, though frustrating, somehow fitting. I've still never figured the place out. It somehow considers itself both the East Coast and the Midwest. I don't count it among the Midwest states because it's on Eastern Standard Time, but that's a line in the sand that only I seem to draw.

A phone call with The D Man goes well. Like most hardcore kids who are old enough to drink, he's more laid back and open to different styles of music than you would think. The D Man is cool, if a little reserved. He doesn't talk much but he's got a lot of good things going for him. Besides having an established label with distribution he's also got a partnership with an agency in Europe. They distribute his records over there as well as book the bands on his label to tour the continent. It is this factor that really moves the needle for us. Europe is a seemingly unattainable touring goal, we don't know anyone who has actually done it. We have friends of friends who have but we've got no way to start even routing something like that, let alone booking it. So we decide to sign.

The contract is for two albums and one extended play single or EP. The EP we already recorded on our own so that's good to go, but we previously promised two of the four tracks to a tiny label in Rhode Island called Contrast Records. It's decided that Contrast will get two songs, "A Newfound Interest In Massachusetts" and "Off The Wagon," for a 7″ single, while The D Man will get the remaining two tracks, "Woodson" and "Second Place," for a different 7″ single and all four of them for CD. Things are set in motion to manufacture these products as soon as we sign the contract. This business of contracts, however, is a new and daunting prospect that I'm not totally comfortable with.

We've procured the services of a lawyer. He works with Boys Life and he's the only entertainment lawyer I've ever heard of around here. I even ask my dad, the hot shot labor lawyer, but he only knows people like that in New York or Los Angeles or Nashville. So this guy is kinda the only game in town.

On the day we are to sign the contract, the lawyer tells us not to. He says that another label, a brother and sister team from Los Angeles, is also interested. I tell him we can't, we've already made a verbal commitment with The D Man. Nothing's been signed, he says. The D Man's contract isn't that great anyway but it doesn't matter. I've given my word, the paperwork is just a formality. I'm nothing if not loyal.

The contract is signed and we are booked into Chicago Recording Company with the producer we want to work with, Bob Weston. Ryan skips class and we wait for him in the parking lot of his high school with the van. Earlier that morning we had run over a large rock and cracked the manifold. The beast still runs but there is a distinct aroma of carbon monoxide hanging in the air. All the way to Chicago we keep the windows down in the cold spring air to let the noxious fumes dissipate.

The singer of my old noise band is now living in Chicago and lets us crash at his place on West Thomas. We spend almost every moment of our two-and-a-half days in town at this prestigious studio in a chaotic marathon session with an indie rock legend. We attempt a synthesizer part but the keyboard is out of tune. We can't seem to get it into the right key. Weston rectifies this by manually slowing down the tape machine until it sounds correct, literally tuning the tape to the song. We only break to eat pizza, watch *The Simpsons,* and sleep. It is a hurried affair and ultimately perfect in its imperfection, nothing if not sincere.

At one point, The D Man comes to the studio and listens to what we've been working on. He says nothing of our progress, but I don't really care. I'm too focused on the task at hand. He buys us dinner like a proper label head should. We dine on cheap pizza devoid of the customary meats we would normally consume. The D Man is a vegetarian and therefore won't buy meat for his clients. This is a dick move, I think to myself as I house a slice of Margherita.

Ryan needs to get back to high school on Monday morning. On the drive back to Kansas City we listen to a cassette of our masterpiece. "Is this any good?" I find myself asking the group, having never had doubt about a recording like this before. We aren't content but we don't have money to fix it, so we're just gonna have to put it out. The D Man doesn't seem to hate it so it goes on the docket. The EP we did with producer Ed Rose back home sounds better than this, though.

Four Minute Mile comes out in the fall and is displayed at the front of the new releases in Recycled Sounds. We're not relegated to the "local" section anymore. A teenage Adrianne Verhoeven brings our LP up to the counter and asks, "Are these guys any good?" "Nah," I tell her. "They're pretty terrible." I don't know if she knows that I'm kidding, and I'm not entirely sure that I am either. She buys the record anyway.

Once we start touring, the lifeblood of our operation becomes merch. For us that means the band's shirts ("soft goods" or "cotton") and then of course music in the form of compact discs and vinyl. Vinyl, which at this time is dead to the mainstream, is still very much a part of the punk rock underground. Between hip hop DJs and our scene it's the only thing keeping the pressing plants alive. It's pretty easy to get a quick turnaround on vinyl, but it gets harder and harder for us to get our wax from The D Man. Sometime after we signed he acquired a distribution company and seems to be prioritizing its needs over ours. If there are only a hundred records left in stock they will be sent to stores and not to us on the road.

I see this as a betrayal and take it very personally. When a shipment of records arrives at a show in Denver and they are all misprints I lose it. Thankfully, somebody listened to the copy of the EP they bought at the show and brought it back to tell us that it was the wrong band. Apparently the pressing plant made a mistake and put another band's songs on our record. I blame the label for this though it's not entirely their fault. We're expected to be thankful to be able to work with them, and they don't appear to be grateful for the hard work we're putting in. We live in our van and on strangers' floors for months with no support from the label at all. We don't ask for much, just enough product to be able to sell so that we can have money for gas and food. We aren't even asking for any kind of tour support.

Tour support is a funny thing, it sounds like a good idea until you do it. You're essentially taking out a loan from the label in order to go on tour. It's easy to misperceive it as a gift but it's actually your money, nothing a record label gives you is free. That's not a complaint it's just a fact, everything is an advance that you'll have to pay back or recoup.

After living hand-to-mouth for years one could be forgiven for thinking of this as the brass ring. To be able to budget for a tour at all, let alone to be in the black at the end of it, is an enticing carrot at the end of the stick. We don't fuck with tour support, we just follow the Black Flag and Mike Watt philosophy, which we have rechristened "Live To Gig, Gig To Live." That pretty much sums it up. The fact that this record label doesn't think that the show is the most important part of this whole process means we've got a problem. Maybe we should start looking for a new place to call home.

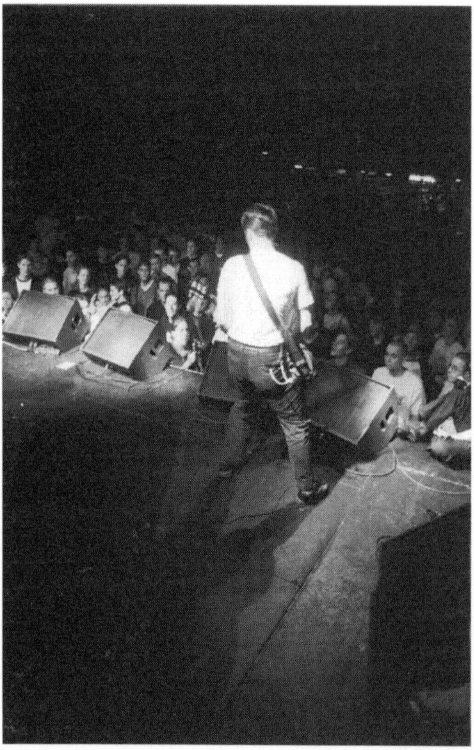

Live To Gig, Gig To Live

I am at a house on the other side of the state line. It's the house where Coalesce practice. Sometimes they put on shows in the basement. Today is the first day of the rest of our lives. The first of many days spent in a van, on the highway, making a racket in basements. Today is the first day we will meet the Champaign band, Braid, in person. They are a bit older and have done this before, they will teach us a lot. But today, they are just another four randos in an old Dodge, playing music to twenty or thirty people in a run-down house on the wrong side of the tracks.

There is an uneasy element at this place. There's a group of men with shaved heads. Not SHARPs, maybe SHARP-adjacent. They are kung fu Buddhists, modern warrior monks, large and tattooed (Bill The Drill is a member) and intimidating. They are also friends with Coalesce. One of them whips a bagel at my head, hitting me in the back of the neck and leaving a welt. I let this transgression go unaddressed because I don't want any piece of this crew. What am I gonna do, fight them?

Aside from the bagel incident the night is uneventful. We arrange the instruments under the loft in the van and head off into the sunrise to our first real show in Minneapolis, a northern middle American staple, birthplace of some of the greats. We play a show there on the floor in a record store. The streets outside have potholes that seem large enough to have been caused by landmines. The weather really does a number on the asphalt here. During our performance my request for hydration is answered with a bottle of caffeinated water, if you can believe such a thing exists. It is more dehydrating than moonshine and does nothing to soothe my ever-deteriorating voice.

We play what would become the first of many gigs at the Fireside Bowl in Chicago, an institution now lost to the ages. They do not close the lanes while the band plays. Our amplifiers are no match for the roll of the ball and the crack of the pins. The stage—oh yeah, an actual stage—is in the bowling room in order to keep minors out of the bar portion of the venue. Inside the bar a jukebox blares at a deafening volume loud enough to be heard over the juvenile racket being performed by us and our peers. Less than ideal conditions, but this place is glorious.

We arrive in a sweltering New York City shirtless with the windows lowered, trying to get a reprieve from the oppressive temperature. A wrong turn, maybe a right turn, puts our van of five half-nude teenage boys right in the center of the Pride festivities. A group of barely clothed and incredibly fit men wave at us. Welcome to the big city, you clueless hayseeds.

There are two shows on the island of Manhattan. The first is at a dive bar that has yet to be ruined by hipsters. Backstage is actually *under* the stage, making it impossible to carry on a conversation during a performance directly overhead. A band from Canada or Australia or somewhere are the headliner. They will be getting the bulk of the cut of the door even though we were the draw. This is the one adults-only event on this trip. There are more youths outside on the sidewalk trying to peek in through the window than there are paying customers inside. Our audience skews young. We are given thirty American dollars, not even enough for gas.

The other thing under the stage is a walk-in cooler. A barback's error has left this beer cave unlocked and unattended. Upset by our financial mistreatment, we decide to compensate ourselves with alcohol, filling our drum case with lagers. The case is beyond heavy and requires four people to carry it. We couldn't be more suspicious, but our heist is a success. Absconding with our prize, we make it back to the apartment where we're staying and revel in our bounty.

The second show on the island is an all-ages matinee at CBGB's, a legendary venue, the kind I get to brag about later. In order to maximize profit, two shows of apparently conflicting scenes are forced together. This is pretty common for us. Back home, since none of the bands really sound alike in Kansas City, we're used to playing with some pretty different acts.

The scene here seems more territorial. The singer of a local hardcore band distributed promotional material for this show mocking us and our tour mates. They seem to think of us as weak. "Another wretched EMO band on tour," am I right? But there are more people here to see us than him, so he can fuck right off as far as we're concerned. An inquiry is made as to whether back in Kansas City we ride cows to work. Firstly, one does not ride a cow, one rides a horse. Secondly, the only person I ever saw ride a horse in town was a dude who performed in the Black rodeo and he was un-fuck-with-able. Next question. We are treated like a curious oddity from a foreign land, exotic in our thrift store and uniform supply aesthetic.

In Maryland we meet The Collector, who lets us stay at his enormous dormitory suite. He asks if we will perform for his university public access television show. We say no, but relent with the promise it will only be available university-wide. It's all available on the information superhighway as of this writing. In this video I have a fever, we have eaten enough spaghetti to kill a horse, and everyone else is drunk. Glad we got that on tape.

We head back north to play a cultural hall in Lawn Guy Land. They won't let us drink in the bar so we buzz secretly in the van. The opener is Atom and His Package, a guy with a drum machine that is as much comedy as anything else. One of us asks The Collector to get some water but he thinks we want a re-up of booze. He fills a water bottle with vodka and the unsuspecting band member chugs it, spitting it out all over the front row. This is even less hydrating than the caffeinated spring water we had on the first night.

We play in Philly at Stalag 13. The venue we were supposed to play got shut down the day before, so we're basically at some grindcore band's rehearsal space. I'm told that they do shows here where they lock the doors, kill the lights and see what happens. There are too many kids so we have to play twice. The first show is hot and wet. We take to the street flushed red and exhausted after our set. We've still got another round of songs to perform. We pop into the bar next door, down a pint and steady ourselves for round two.

This is Philly, so there are fights. The door guy, who, fun fact, never takes off his Venom shirt even during sex (not sure why I'm told that), bashes a few meatheads who attempt to manhandle this new contingent. Teenagers have started appearing at more and more shows and they don't know the rules. These are not our rules, they are established by the scene that has adopted us. They are exclusionary and hyper-masculine and not our scene whatsoever. This disconnection starts to come into focus a bit later on when we play a show in Goleta, California, promoted by a writer for a hardcore magazine. We seem to be the pop band, or E-word band, that hardcore kids, grindcore kids, metal kids and other aggressive music fans are allowed to like. Not sure what that's about.

On the way to Rhode Island I have a revelation. We can probably do this for real, it doesn't have to just be a summer job. School will always be there later. Most of the guys agree. Jim might take some convincing, he does have an art school scholarship after all. That night we play in a house owned by a teetotaler who released one of our records. He put X's in the artwork without our consent. He makes us vegan rice crispy treats, which are gross. Nice enough guy, but kinda pushy with his politics.

We set up in the basement. Braid sets up directly in front of us across the musty underground room. We trade songs back and forth, giving the attendees whiplash as they have to spin around every three minutes lest they miss the start of either of our compositions. To us it is hilarious, to the audience it is irritating. That night we try to sneak ten fully grown men into one hotel room. It is a luxury of last resort after we fail to find a floor to sleep on. We are caught by the hotel staff. I spend the night in the van, sweating on the loft.

We play Bloomington, Indiana, on the night Princess Diana dies. Ryan storms off when I refer to him as Napoleon to the crowd. That one's on me, dick move. The promoter's house has a half pipe in the garage and Jim takes a spin. Buzzkill me warns him that he's gonna fucking break his arm or something and then we'll have to cancel the whole tour. He just gives me the finger.

Cape Fear, North Carolina, in a used clothing store. The kids here are all into nut smacking, grazing testicles with the back of their hands. Even the girls do it. That's a hell of a way to say hello. I can't hear a goddamn word the whole set, which isn't really that uncommon at these sorts of shows. The vocal PA at a house show is often not loud enough to be heard over our amplifiers. After our set, the store owner walks over to the power box and turns it on. Guess nobody noticed before now. The gang stocks up on honey-flavored smokes because they are wicked cheap in this tobacco-friendly state, and they need burrito money. We're only living on five dollars a day, after all.

Florida, not sure where. The humidity causes some of the gang to go shirtless just like in New York. This will come to be called a "Florida Shirt," meaning no shirt at all. There's all these fuck bugs everywhere, each pair of the flying insects joined together in coitus. The club is in a strip mall and the whole show is plugged into one outlet on the side of the very small stage. Power strips plugged into power strips electrifying the amplifiers as well as the PA. I'm surprised the house lights are even on a different breaker. In a fit of enthusiasm, some random kid runs into the outlet and unplugs the entire show. Ryan keeps playing, the drummer is always the last to know when the power goes out.

In Atlanta we must be in a rough part of town, because the club actually has a security guard and he's got a gun. I start a song that Jim doesn't want to play and he spits in my face from across the stage. I laugh and keep playing. He is honor-bound to finish the song. There are rules after all. In Alabama we play with a band from Boston that I know through Honey White. They've recruited our old drummer, The Sculptor. This is awkward, haven't seen him in a while. He is apologetic and we toast to it, he's not a teetotaler anymore, which is probably why he's chilled the fuck out.

Austin has a festival called South By something-or-other. We play the second floor of a bar. Every nook and cranny apparently is turned into a venue this time of year. The show is all ages but you must have a festival laminate to get in. We befriend some local fans and sneak them into the show, telling the security that they are band members. The goons either are too busy or really don't care, but it becomes a fun game of what random instruments we can think of to add to our ensemble. Horn, flute, triangle, we must have gotten in twenty extra people.

Dallas brings us to a Christian club. This was the only all-ages option in Deep Ellum, though it's at the ass end of the strip. The owner asks us to not swear onstage, but fuck that. Our crowd has been getting increasingly younger lately and they rush the stage when we start to play. The owner, seeing that there is now extra space in the back because of the diminutive size of the young patrons, allows more people to purchase tickets and come into the club, drastically exceeding capacity.

This place is a sauna, the sweat of the patrons condensing on the ceiling and then dripping back onto the stage. We attempt to mop up the recycled sweat but the floor is still wet. We slide around, often slipping onto our asses as we perform. Outside afterward we pant with exhaustion and curse the owner. Of course the Christian club would be the greediest, the least concerned with the well-being of the patrons. It's just what Jesus would have done, right?

105

The discovery that there is a Christian punk rock underground is unnerving to me. I have nothing against organized religion in general, and I'm not an atheist even at this young and angry age, but I got into this to get away from these Bible thumpers. They never accepted me and I never wanted their support. Over the years I have found this scene to be particularly predatory and insidious. Predatory because it feeds on power and control. Insidious because it preys on people who believe that they are on the side of the light, their faith blinding them into thinking that they aren't being taking advantage of. There is a special place in hell for people who use the teachings of the man from Nazareth for their own gain.

Flint, Michigan, stuck in a blizzard. Driving to a skate shop at fifteen miles an hour. We're never gonna get there at this speed, and why would anyone go to a show in this weather? Michiganders come from sturdy stock, they are basically Canadian. There's a decent turnout of parka'd youths and they are ready to emote. The Arizona band we're on tour with take party drug muscle relaxers before they play, all of them but the drummer. They got the drugs when we all went to Tijuana together on a day trip from San Diego. We all came back with knives, they came back with pills. Their set is a slog. The furious and sober man on the kit struggles to slow down enough to keep up with their drug-induced reduction in tempo.

Wilkes Barre, Pennsylvania, at a festival in an old fire station. Coalesce is here. They've taken to closing their set with a Townshend-like gear smashing and James, their drummer, throws a floor tom into the crowd, hitting a girl in the head. He is immediately apologetic to her but defiant of the promoter. She recovers and he pays a penance by getting her merch from many of the other bands. The promoter says he should be arrested but he just sucks on his dart and calmly responds, "Haven't you ever seen us play before?" I laugh in spite of myself, I'm just glad the girl's not hurt. The show will become the stuff of legend. Some will say he killed that girl with his floor tom on that day, but that's not true. She did have a lump though.

Columbus, Ohio, at another goddamn festival. There's a hardcore band that is more socialist substance than sonic style and they play right before us. We played basketball together one time in their hometown, so I assume we're at least on the same page. Somehow they've turned the whole fest into some sort of sharing circle, passing the mic around so people can tell their stories of abuse. I'm a child of recovery, I know that support groups are a net positive, but that's not what this is. This is a fest, not talk therapy.

We just want to play, we need this as much as anyone. I've always subscribed to, and benefitted from, the therapeutic aspects of both playing and listening to loud music. For the brief time that we can make noise and flail around and sing there is nothing wrong with the world. All worry disappears in that tiny moment. This is our therapy, that is how we and everyone in attendance "work through it," whatever "it" is.

It's decided that the show will go on and the sharing circle will take place in the parking lot. A line is drawn in the sand. Our friends in another band decide not to play out of solidarity. It is awkward and uncomfortable but by our second song the entire group in the parking lot is back inside singing along. This is our support group, we are with our people, they are screaming the words and literally pounding their chests.

We roll back into Kansas City at five in the morning. There is something wonderful about the off hours. The world is quiet, only a few cars on the road. I drop off The Popes at their house, Jim at his dad's place, and then park the van in front of my apartment. We just did a whole tour with no incident, but it's the moment we get home that the van gets broken into. They don't clean us out, just take a couple of guitars, including Rob's beautiful seafoam green Fender P bass. This city can't be trusted.

It's strange, the juxtaposition of how much we've grown on this adventure and how little the city has changed. The coffee shop I would hide out in when I skipped class in high school makes my usual drink just like always. They haven't even noticed I was gone.

Everyone is the star of their own movie and nobody wants to be reminded that they are stuck. That's the problem, it's easy to get stuck here. I've heard it called "The Golden Handcuffs" or, my personal favorite, "The Velvet Rut." It's cheap here, easy to get work and seemingly harder and harder to leave.

We are an anomaly in our hometown. People don't seem to be proud of our accomplishments. If anything, they seem annoyed that bands passing through ask about us. In our scene we are the only cultural reference point for this town. We fly the flag of our hometown proudly but our hometown doesn't fly ours. We are written up in the local paper, my grandmother keeps the article on her fridge until the day she dies. The entertainment rag, however, pans us hard. I assume it's tall poppy syndrome. Who do we think we are, actually being successful? We're a touring punk band, we aren't playing stadiums but it's all the same to them, I guess. It seems like we are othered for having the sheer audacity to leave.

It's Dark Out Lately

It's dark out lately, has been for a while now. It's currently forty seven minutes past 3:00 a.m. and I am at the wheel. From now until sunrise I am the captain of this Black Mariah, its bowels filled with instruments, clothing and fools. They slumber now, getting whatever inebriated version of rest can be achieved at this velocity. We are, at this tired hour, long-haul truckers. We are bound to a book of maps conveniently titled *Atlas*. It is our bible, our guide, and our only clue to where in the ever-living fuck we are. Somewhere in Idaho, hours past takeoff, and more hours shy of our destination.

We left town, if you can call it that, two hundred and forty minutes ago. Sleepy college hamlet, Mormon school. Lily white, free from crime and culture. A friend of a friend of The Brothers knows a student. Five grown men going into her dorm room got the authorities called. Expulsion was averted when inquires led not to lascivious carnal acts but rather the use of the toilet. We were off to a good start.

We are troubadours and these are our stages. We vacillate between the high altars and flooded basements. We welcome both with the same enthusiasm of fools who don't know better. For we don't know better, we are building the boat as it sails. This ship is barely held together, and honestly, so are we.

It's so dark, so quiet. I've been riding the dial on the AM side of the radio to find Art Bell. Usually, from about 1:00 a.m. to 5:00 a.m. you can find him if you surf long enough. It's never a strong signal but when it starts to crack you can slide into the next region's broadcast. It's a fitting companion for this sort of travel. Lonely, isolated conspiracy addicts desperate for attention. Grabbing at their fifteen minutes of fame and then falling back into obscurity. We're not so different, you and me.

The friend of a friend of The Brothers books us in a pizza parlor. Not the first pie shop we've played. There was one in Bakersfield that ended in a meth head fight. This one, however, has one microphone but no stand. I wear two hats. I carry a guitar as a prop, strumming it from time to time. More importantly, I mangle words into a microphone with great volume and purpose while playing said instrument. Needless to say, I need a fucking mic stand.

Solution: grab a box of vinyl records from the van and duct tape a broom handle to it. Then affix an empty toilet paper roll to said handle and you've got a MacGyver'd cradle to rest a microphone. Said stand will last for upwards of thirty minutes of high-energy octave chord rock as long as there are no disruptions, but there are disruptions. These kids are sheltered, repressed, horny. They need an outlet to blow off steam. We are the best they are going to get. One particularly fit specimen starts to "mosh" by doing push-ups on the floor in front of me. We just keep playing, it's all we know how to do.

We can at least take some solace in this. It's better than not having a gig at all. Non-show days take the same amount of expenses without the income. Plus, maybe we gave the kids, especially these kids, a good time. Maybe we gave them a distraction from their anxieties. A release from society and their parents' expectations of them. I'm projecting, I know. It helps to make it seem like this gig had some purpose. Some band has to be your gateway drug to punk rock, maybe that push-up kid is the next Kurt Cobain. Who's to say?

But now, it's quiet. I can't find the radio signal so we travel on in silence. At the first sign of fatigue I need to get some coffee. But, there is no reprieve, we are on a dark stretch. A road so remote you can use the high beams on the interstate. It's a very good place to blunt force trauma a deer or any of its cloven-hoofed kin. A friend's band hit a moose somewhere in these parts. It demolished the passenger side of the vehicle. It was a splatter show of blood and bone. Luckily no humans were hurt so they pulled into the parking lot of a fast food restaurant known for hamburgers and clowns. A group of kindergarteners on a milkshake-shaped slide started to scream at the sight. Traumatized by the carnage, even in the Mountain West.

Finally I find an oasis, a two-pump station, a throwback still common in these parts. This is no Flying J, this is mom-and-pop. They don't take credit, not that we have any anyway. Ours is a cash business, under the table. I hitch up the Mariah and saunter in. I actually walk like a cowboy until I get my land legs. My muscles have mildly atrophied from being stationary these last few hours. The outside is lit by neon, adverts for piss beer and chewin' tobacco.

Upon entry I must close my eyes to adjust to the garish fluorescent lighting. The coffee station houses an old school church basement percolator, the kind they use for twelve-step meetings or funerals. The smell is a chemical weapon that surely has been outlawed by the Geneva Convention but I pour the hot black syrup into a Styrofoam cup. I ponder the irony of pouring a poisonous liquid into a receptacle which is made of, essentially, poison. Which is worse for the planet, the coffee or the cup? Probably the coffee.

The noxious brew was most likely made the previous morning. It is essentially battery acid, but that's honestly what I need. This is a night drive, not a pajama party. The distress it wreaks on my gastrointestinal tract is just one of many hazards of this job. After this tour I go to a gut doctor who suggests I might suffer from something called gastritis. I think that's just egghead for too much night-drive gas station coffee and seventy-nine-cent bean burritos.

We each live on five dollars a day, that Chihuahua's dollar menu our only sustenance. That, and Chex Mix. Night-drive coffee is a band expense, though, so this doesn't eat into my burrito money. It's the cost of doing business. I pass over the impulse displays of brightly colored pills and small bottles of saccharine go-go juice. I don't partake in the more efficient stimulants like smokes, yellow jackets or proper amphetamines. I gotta stick with coffee—black, no sugar, at least twelve hours old.

With the poison in tow, the engine roars to life and we ship off again into the night. We're getting into a particularly rural stretch now, not a sign of civilization in several miles. I tried slapping my own face to stay awake but the masochism wasn't my bag, I was pulling my punches. I start running my palm in circles on the thigh of my black jeans, unknowingly transferring the dye to my hand. I rub my tired eyes and at our next respite I am told I look like a raccoon.

I wash off my accidental war paint and take my place back behind the wheel. That goddamn "dead or alive" song comes on the radio. God, I fucking hate that song. There are two circles of hell that Virgil didn't include in Dante's *Inferno*. One is someone incessantly trying to tune a Moog synthesizer, and the other is a constant loop of Bon Jovi's "Wanted Dead Or Alive." The video plays in the background and all you can do is pray for death.

The metaphor of musical traveler as cowboy is belabored at best. It's really a dead horse, and an inaccurate one at that. We are not gauchos, we are pirates, we are mercenaries. We arrive, we lay waste and we leave, hopefully with all of your riches. Then, in the darkness, we are alone with our thoughts. Outside of the show we're just Vikings asking for directions, barbarians waiting to use the pay phone.

I'm willing to bet the scenery is beautiful. I wouldn't know because it's dark like a terror out there. The gang wouldn't know because they are passed out. Finally, I find Art Bell, Coast To Coast AM, the conspiracy theorist's conspiracy theorist. Everyone is welcome, no holds barred, but the man won't just believe you, you have to convince him that your particular brand of crazy just might be the government mind control moon landing hoax that you know it is.

Jeffery from Tucson, long time listener, first time caller, speaks up. He just wants to let you know that, well, he's The Antichrist. "Really?" the host replies. "That's not a very Antichrist thing to say. Thanks for calling." Sam from Reno lowered a tape recorder down a well and now has audio proof of people screaming in hell. Why would he lie about something like that? What is it about the desert that lures these types? Or is it madness that sends someone to live in the desert? I hate the desert. Fuck sand, give me trees.

We're heading to my favorite part of the country, the Northwest. I've been a grunge-loving, flannel in the summer time, Midwest poseur since back in high school. I long for what Dale Cooper called a "Damn fine cup of coffee, black as midnight on a moonless night." Give me rain, give me green trees, mountains, and junkies, I guess?

Not everything is as romantic as you think. The Northwest is so isolated. It's the Perth or Dubai of the US—it takes for fucking ever to get there, but it's magical once you do. Its isolation forces people to be self-reliant. It is the early days of the dot-com bubble and the world is not as flat as it soon will be. This part of the world has its own language, its own scene. They give little fuck about what's happening out East or anything south on this coast.

There's a different kind of redneck out here. One that has more to do with trees than cows. Same sort of mentality, though, put on your boots and get your work done. Keep the feds out of my house and keep your commie pinko bullshit to yourself. I can handle that, we've got similar shit kickers back home.

We pilgrimage to Snoqualmie Falls, Angelo Badalamenti's *Soundtrack From Twin Peaks* on the stereo, Julee Cruise's voice haunting the forest where the owls are not what they seem. The cafe is not the same. Apparently just weeks prior it was bought and transformed by the new owners into a theme diner based around that Warner Bros. parakeet. I really don't get adults who adore, even base their identity around, children's cartoon characters. It seems infantile. Don't get me started on the cult of that fucking mouse. What in the hell is that about?

I order a damn...mediocre cup of coffee. Brown as the newly felled trees on the trucks in the lot. The falls were majestic, the diner is a downer. Life's about managing expectations, I guess. Everybody back in the van, we've still got an hour to go. Seattle, the Emerald City, calls out to us like the siren in a certain coffee chain's logo.

"Wake up, do you smell syrup?" The sickly sweet aroma fills the cab of the Econoline. Shit, that means there's another leak in the radiator and the antifreeze is burning. It's only a matter of time before we overheat and do some real damage to this beast. We've already replaced so many parts we could have bought a whole new cooling system twice over by now.

Well, all there is to do now is pray, and that's not really my bag. Windows down, air con turned off, no more stops until we can get to the city. We'll need to find a phone book and look up auto shops and hope to hell that one of them is kind enough to get us in today. If that's even possible, we'll be charged an exorbitant rush fee, assuming they can even get the parts. Best case scenario, we're waiting around for several hours in an industrial part of town far from any civilization or food. If our luck holds then we'll be able to get to the venue by doors, or, in a worse-case scenario, stage time. The handful of times we've rolled up just as the last band finished and loaded directly onto the stage to play have been stressful. Technically the worst-case scenario would be missing the gig entirely. As long as we can make it maybe we can even afford to pay for this repair.

The mechanic inquires about the two-by-eight inch piece of lumber that lives where our front bumper should be. Well, my younger brother borrowed the van to move into a new apartment and got into a fender bender with a parked car.

A friend Jim and I work with at the fancy library said we could pass Kansas City auto inspection with a wooden bumper. Surely this can't be true, can it? That's the most Boogan thing I've ever heard of. So we try it, and hot diggity shit it actually works. We pass inspection, at a significant savings no less.

The mechanic is impressed with our ingenuity, then delivers the mixed news. Several hundred dollars, but it's only gonna take a couple of hours to get us up and rolling again. However, it's a temporary fix, he says, a Band-Aid. "Ultimately you're gonna need to replace the whole thing." Well, that ain't gonna happen any time soon, old timer, so just patch the bitch up and we'll be on our way.

I am unprepared for the Seattle Zombie Walk. Though some of the best bands from this town have either struggled with or died from heroin addiction, the sheer volume of homeless junkies is staggering. The show tonight is at a recreation center, there is a needle exchange in the bathroom. I have an abundance of clean needles for myself, but I do take advantage of the biohazard bin and discard my empties. There's something depressing about injecting my insulin here, it kinda takes all the humor out of the joke that I do needle drugs at punk shows.

I don't usually have access to proper needle disposal on the road. I don't want to just throw them in the regular trash bin. I've heard stories about people like me getting busted for possession until it can be explained to the authorities that these are not fun drugs, they are just to keep me alive. Plus, I'd hate for a desperate soul to use one of my spent soldiers that may have insulin residue, that could kill a man. So I walk around with an impressive collection of dirty syringes until I can get home. Minimum three to five shots a day and that starts to add up over a month. Going through immigration back into the States after our first tour of Europe took some 'splainin'. Per usual, nobody really knows about my disease. I keep it so close to the vest that I think even my coworkers forget about it. It's only when there is an emergency that it really ever comes up.

It's rare, because I try to head it off before it happens, but I have had very low blood sugars onstage in the past. Our shows are a pretty aerobic workout, I am often drowning in sweat from performing. But once in a while my heart will race and I can tell this is more than just endorphins. I've taken to keeping a bottle of apple or orange juice on the floor next to my amp. If no such beverage can be procured then a full sugar cola will work in a pinch. As soon as the song ends I give the signal that I'm gonna need a minute and slam the whole fucking thing in one gulp. Jim vamps—he loves to talk, thankfully—until I can regain my composure. The juice is better not because it's faster but because it isn't carbonated. I do still have to sing. I've mastered the art of getting through a chorus and then leaning far back to release the impending and offending belch off mic. It is an uncomfortable procedure to say the least.

We've got a friend in town called J-Bone who can put us up for the night. He was in bands back home but now he's tech-bubble rich. He works for some start-up and he's getting bonuses in company stock. Within a year they will be worthless and he'll be broke, but tonight he buys the drinks. I tease him that he still owes me a hundred dollars from a bet several years ago, wherein he was confident he could get us signed to the label his band was on. Glad he didn't. Like all these Seattle start-ups, that label doesn't exist anymore either.

Short drive to Portland, incredibly long overnight drive through the mountains to San Francisco. We've got a real gig at a real club there, opening for the band from Richmond. Sold out show, good times for Avail. Afterwards I am shown the financial breakdown by the Richmond band. It is in this moment that I learn the biggest difference between playing basements with your friends and real shows: the headliner makes all the money. It's not unfair, I'm not upset, just somewhat taken aback by the difference between everyone's wages for the night. It makes sense, it's their show, they are the draw, we're just happy to be here. Thank you for the illuminating, if not painful, teaching moment.

We are in an industrial area of southern California. I think we are in Los Angeles, but we very much are not. The club, if you wanna call it that, is down the street from the second oldest Taco Bell in the country. We make the pilgrimage. We have to, The Bell is our church, the highest height of our culinary experience. We dine and it is delicious. There is a guy at the show who is interested in managing us, I'm not even entirely sure what he means. Managing us for what? Our career, he says plainly. Career? I'm twenty years old, who's thinking about a career? We take his card, he's gonna come to Kansas City and take us out to dinner. No need for a meal tonight, we're already plump with rehydrated pinto beans and fire sauce.

We play Arizona on Halloween at Jimmy Eat World's rehearsal space. Desperate for costumes, we buy a six pack of black women's tights at a supermarket. We'll be bank robbers for Samhain. I quickly learn that attempting to vocalize loudly from inside of a stocking is a messy affair. I rip off the disguise, my face covered in my own saliva. I reappropriate the fabric as a towel and get myself presentable. That took all of two songs, guess I'm the bank robber in the crew that gets made.

It's Sunday night which means it's "Roadie Friday" since we don't have a show the next day. Monday shows are the worst and should be avoided at all costs. We spend the day in Phoenix and hit up a cool local record store that's in a strip mall. The Photographer has given me the number of a booking agent we'll call Mr. Happy who is interested in working with us. At this point, I've booked all the tours myself but am tired of it. He was working for the Promise Ring but they apparently fired him because he was too mean. That's perfect for me, I'm sick of us getting fucked over by shady promoters or house show kids who didn't remember to charge at the door.

At the pay phone outside of the record store I punch in the 917 area code and hold up the dialer. A dialer is a small handheld device about the size of a television remote with a speaker on it. It stores phone numbers by making the tones that the pay phone makes whenever you push the buttons. Instead of carrying around an address book and manually entering the digits, one can keep all their important phone numbers in the dialer. The Photographer knows a guy who can swap out a chip in the dialer and it will make the sound of a quarter being deposited, thus tricking a pay phone into giving one free long-distance calls. It's a touring essential.

The dialer sounds the tones and Mr. Happy picks up. He speaks in short sentences, never using any more words than are absolutely necessary. His voice is deep and gruff and hardened in a way that only native New Yorkers' voices are. He tells me he likes the band but he'll have to see us play first before he'll work with us. I respect that. A lesser agent would have taken us on the merit of our rising popularity, but he wants to make sure anyone he's gonna represent can bring the goods live.

I tell him we'll be at Coney Island High for CMJ next month and we agree to meet. I tell him we need someone to book the next US leg while we're on tour in Europe at the beginning of next year. He doesn't think that should be a problem. He takes ten percent, just of our cut of the gate, nothing else. Seems like a fair deal and we hang up. He doesn't seem so mean to me, just to the point. I have no concerns that he isn't gonna like us live, at our shows we are out for blood.

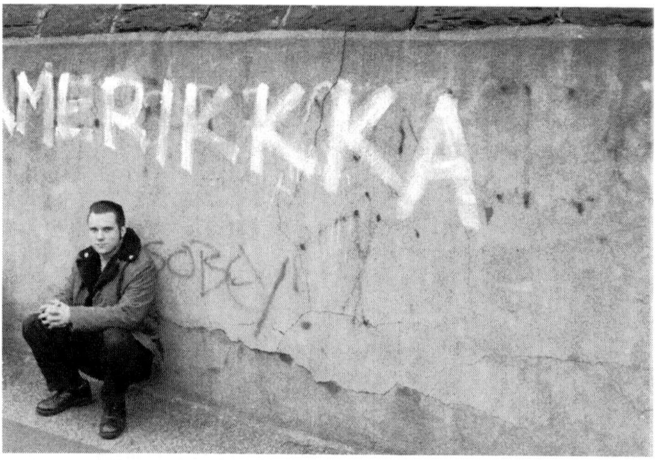
MERIKKA

Dollars To Deutschmarks

We are driving dangerously fast along the interstate. I am riding shotgun, white knuckling the "oh shit" bar with all of my strength. James is driving though he isn't in the band yet, he's just a new friend. He loves to drive, it combines his three loves: going fast, listening to loud music and smoking. His window comes down every twenty minutes to puff on a dart. Later, in the pocket technology era, he will do all this while constantly texting. That's how he lives, as if life has no consequences. It's a miracle any of us are still alive.

We are racing to St. Louis, the River City, past the Casino Queen all the way to the airport. Why drive an extra four hours when there is a perfectly suitable runway in Kansas City? Because the flights are cheaper and we are not footing the bill. That's not entirely true, anything that gets "paid" for by the record label comes out of our cut. I don't fully understand this yet, but I will learn. Painfully, we will all learn.

We are flying to Germany—Frankfurt to be more precise. There we will meet Braid, as well as two representatives from our record label. One is a comedian, the other is humorless. The flight is uneventful. It's not until our second trip that the plane will get struck by lightning. No news is good news as far as air travel is concerned. We are the first to arrive in Europe. I am immediately uneasy about the security wielding semi-automatic machine guns. I thought we were the country that was the horniest for firearms but I've never seen an American airport cop with an AR15.

Exchange dollars for Deutschmarks, I need coffee immediately, but first baggage, customs, immigration, all also uneventful. Nothing lost or broken, no problems getting past the feds. We do not, however, have work permits. Foolishly, even though we are carrying several guitars, drums and cymbals, we decide to try our luck claiming to be tourists. To my surprise it actually works. This ridiculous plan will work country after country, except in the ones where it doesn't. Britain is already being discussed as a potential problem. They are, apparently, sticklers for paperwork.

After reuniting with Braid and the label reps we head out of the airport to meet our driver. He has the same handle as two others in our motley crew so he's given the nickname "Action Rob." He's a pleasant enough Englishman, which may prove advantageous when we arrive at that island. He walks us to the Sprinter, an eight-passenger Mercedes affair with an impenetrable wall between the band and the instruments. No loft, guess we're sleeping upright on this trip. The other whip is a modest midsize sedan. There are thirteen of us total, eight in the van, five in the sedan. This is utility touring, designed for efficiency, not for comfort. Six weeks we will live in these vehicles, rotating who has to sleep in the Sprinter each night to guard the gear. It's gonna be a long month and a half.

Our first stop is to pick up all the backline equipment and any merchandise that we had made in-country to supplement the shirts we smuggled over in our luggage. We find ourselves in a residential suburb of Frankfurt with streets so narrow it's hard to navigate with the Sprinter. A warm German man greets us at the front door of his house and invites us inside. It's a modest, what I would call middle-class place complete with large television and fish tank. Bachelor, I assume. We are shuttled to his office, where he has a larger-than-life self-portrait above his desk. I sign the rental agreement as his larger omnipotent self gazes down at me in judgment.

We are taken to the garage, where we gather two Marshall 4x12 speaker cabinets, two Marshall JCM series tube amplifiers, one

Ampeg 8×10 bass cabinet, one Gallien-Krueger solid state bass amplifier, and one four-piece black Tama drum kit complete with cymbals, hardware and cases. We finagle a kind of Tetris to get everything into the back compartment of the Sprinter and wave to the creepy painting as we walk out the door.

The first show is at a youth center somewhere outside of Düsseldorf. Thankfully, the place is packed, the Germans are aware of us and seem to be appreciative. They are not as aware of Braid. This difference is the reason why we signed a bad record deal in the first place, the distribution in Europe. Braid's label has the UK covered, but there's very little of theirs available on the mainland, primarily just imports or bootlegs. German-made bootlegs of punk and hardcore records are apparently a lucrative business over here.

First noticeable difference, the club actually feeds the bands and crew. Both snacks at load-in and a proper family dinner after sound check, before doors. It's quite civilized. We make our racket and leave the stage. The crowd is chanting for more. What are we gonna do? We've never been asked to do an encore before, we just played all the songs we know. We are informed that it would be considered disrespectful to the patrons if we refused to play another song. There are rules after all. We scramble and walk back out to play a song we haven't rehearsed in over a year. It's hardly a perfect performance but it satiates the rabid audience. From now on, we'll be sure to leave at least one song out of the set for this sort of occasion.

Second noticeable difference, the club provides us with a place to sleep. Granted it's hostel-style bunks, shared bathroom down the hall, but it's still an actual bed. In the States we'd been taking to the mic to ask the crowd if anyone had a floor we could crash on. We will learn that, like tonight's club, many of these venues will have housing on site. Therefore we don't have to load out until the next morning. What a glorious gift to not have to do the manual labor of load-out after the show. To be able to rest and not "hump gear" while you're soaking wet during the brutal German winter.

Braid brings Paul Drake, The Photographer, to sling their cotton. He's a little older than us and significantly more hardened. He is adamant, almost with religious zealotry, that we waste not one minute of our time on this continent. He does not care how tired I am or about any of our states of mental health. We are here, we know full well that we may never have this opportunity again, and we are not going to waste it. We are going to see every possible inch of every goddamn city that we perform in.

His fervor is infectious, if a little overwhelming. But he's right of course, I won't waste this, I won't waste the future opportunities either. His attitude fundamentally changes my thinking. I'd never really thought of this as fleeting before. I am a child, I only think about the present and maybe six months into the future. This is the first opportunity to think of this job, this life of touring, as a bizarre gift not to be taken for granted.

The second night in Germany, someone throws a sounding grenade into the back door of the venue. What the fuck is a sounding grenade? It's apparently the grenade version of rubber bullets, something intended to frighten and hurt but not murder. The explosion happens very close to Rob, who now has a constant ringing in his ears. We'll all have that eventually, such is the life. Boxers get cauliflowers, musicians get tinnitus. No one is really hurt, but the threat of Germans with grenades is a bit off-putting.

We are performing in what was, until fairly recently, East Germany. When the people here speak English, they are more difficult to understand than their Western brethren. The kids in Berlin speak better 'merican than we do. But here in the former East Germany, we might as well be in Russia, I don't know what the fuck anyone is saying. I get by, I'm learning how to be a traveler. I point at pictures of food, and get the subtle hint that you're supposed to tip the gas station bathroom attendant. This is not optional and not how it is done back home. In the States I do not have to dip into my burrito money, or in this case kebab money, in order to take a shit.

We walk along the Berlin Wall and visit Checkpoint Charlie, which now has a gift shop. It's only been eight years since the Soviets fell, but it feels like an eternity ago. I've heard stories of punk bands smuggling themselves into the Eastern Bloc even during the height of the Cold War. I wouldn't have the stones for something like that. Those bands are anarchists mostly.

Wanna hear a joke? How many anarchists does it take to change a light bulb? Answer: anarchists can't change anything. Action Rob doesn't think this joke is funny. He wants to smash the state but he still lives on the dole. He changes the subject, singing the little tune he's written, *"I've got scabies, they itch like fuck,"* and I hope that he's kidding but I'm not sure that he is.

The next morning I wake up in the van as it rolls into Prague during the sunrise. I am not prepared for this, I didn't know anything about this place other than it used to be one country and then woke up one day and was cut in half. It's foggy and gothic, it's as if Tim Burton had built the Disney Magic Kingdom to his own twisted specifications. I am in awe, walking to the Cathedral we learn the statues adorning it are depictions of sinners being hurled from atop the wall. This place is metal as hell!

We learn that everything is still so old because nobody really bombed the shit out of it during the war. It's relatively free from American influence, at least it is today. There will be more and more McDonald's every time we come back to visit. But today it's twenty-five cents for the best Pilsner in the world and you can still buy hardcore pornography from street vendors. Apparently absinthe is legal here as well as prostitution. I'm not really into either of those things, I barely drink and am hopelessly codependent on my girlfriend, but whatever floats your boat. We perform at a club named after James Bond and the bass amp shits the bed, so the bass goes directly into the PA instead of an amp. We play the whole show not being able to hear it, ignorant of how it sounds in the house.

We've pressed a special limited edition version of the split 7" we released with Braid in the States. It's a European tour exclusive complete with a map of the continent as the cover art. An irritated Czech fan who's a few Budvars deep confronts us about the outdated map on the record. It still features Czechoslovakia, which, again, only split up eight years ago. We can play the stupid American card because, in this instance anyway, that's what we are. A skinhead steals our merch cash and our handsome merch guy jumps over the table to punch him and retrieve the only money we really have. All the gig proceeds are being wired to the booking agent. No idea when it will make it to us.

We have to go through border crossings almost every day. We need to exchange currencies, too. We're really getting fucked on the exchange rates and fees, having to do this so often. At the Austrian border we are forced to unload the entire van, all our instruments littering the side of the highway. Todd, the bass player in Braid, has put all his multivitamins into a Ziploc bag and it looks like he's a drug smuggler. He is confronted by the border guards and, not speaking their language, he flexes his arms like a body builder and says "to make you strong." They laugh at him and tell us to fill the van back up. Nothing to see here, be on your way.

Croatia is its own adventure. They only declared independence seven years ago and the conflict that followed is over, I think? Like usual, we don't have work permits and we wait at the border as Action Rob tries to negotiate our way into the country. We call the promoter and she tells us to drive to a different border crossing, they aren't going to let us in here. We drive about an hour out of our way to this second checkpoint, where we are surprised to see the promoter waiting for us. She has shocking electric blue hair that is even more pronounced surrounded by all this Soviet grey. She nods to the border guard and we are allowed through. She offers no explanation, and I don't ask.

There are potholes in the highway. I don't know if this is from the weather or the war. Zagreb is beautiful and the kids are hungry for us. They are hungry for anything. Nobody comes to Croatia, but they are missing out. It's somewhat comforting that appreciative people in out-of-the-way cities aren't an exclusively American phenomenon.

In Italy we play a squat in a beach town during the winter. There is no one here. It's winter at the beach. There is a basketball hoop in the parking lot and we engage in a friendly game of HORSE to pass the time. I throw the ball at full force right into the chest of Ryan because I'm angry that he's smoking weed before we play. He tackles me to the ground. I've said it before and I'll say it again: The Brothers are not to be fucked with. That one's on me.

We're fed cold pizza with corn kernels on it. The fuck? Even before my foodie awakening I at least know that Italy is known for its culinary prowess. This is garbage, what a disappointment. Our accommodations for the evening are to sleep on the stage after the club closes. I volunteer to take the van shift. I'm not nearly drunk enough to sleep on a hard wooden stage that reeks of old beer and cigarettes. What a glamorous life we lead.

We approach the border into Switzerland. Action Rob warns of the troubles he's had getting in and out of this country. Comically, when we get to the checkpoint they interrogate the guitarist of Braid, who calmly states, "I'm sorry sir, I don't speak gibberish." Mortified, we wait for the guard's response, but he doesn't seems to understand us and we are allowed to pass.

In Zurich we are taken to a mansion that has been squatted in and now owned by a punk collective. Apparently it was abandoned during the war and these enterprising young folks jumped on it. They've built a skateboard half pipe in the drawing room and restored the glamorous dining room to its former glory. We all sit around an enormous table that easily seats twenty-plus and are treated to home-cooked veggie lasagna. They are incredibly generous. I ask about Swiss food. Other than fondue, chocolate and cheese, what else is Switzerland known for? I am told "Switzerland is just known for being perfect." Alright. Asked and answered, I guess.

In Paris we stay at the apartment of a young bootlegger. He is a tape trader, his home is filled with VHS tapes of concerts, movies, pornography, you name it. He has snuff films, or so he claims, bestiality as well. He's excited to share, popping in a video of a woman being mounted by a dog. During one particularly grainy video I have to inquire what exactly we are watching. "I believe he is fucking a chicken," he responds, unimpressed as the audible clucking comes into focus. This is too much for me, I'm gonna go to bed. The gang descends into the night, they aren't going to waste their one night in *Paree*. I steady myself and get rest. England is coming, and I know that's going to be a trial. Even if we can make it into the country it's not gonna be nearly as cushy a gig as we've had so far.

We drive through the night to the port of Calais and wait for the sun to rise. Action Rob and I keep ourselves awake by playing a name game, the first letter of a celebrity's last name must become the first letter of the next celebrity's first name. As we get tired, the parameters of our game narrow. First it is musicians, then guitar players, then heavy metal guitar players, and by the time we whittle it down to New Wave of British Heavy Metal lead (not rhythm) guitar players the sun is coming up. It is time to board the ferry to Dover.

The ferry from Calais to Dover doesn't take very long, and if you feed the seagulls when you depart they will follow the boat all the way to England. I love the ferry, it might be my favorite part of touring. We sit out on the deck and watch France disappear in the distance, we dine in the cafeteria on both baguette with Brie and beans on toast. The pub is open and we have pints at 7:00 a.m., putting coins into the video jukebox to watch classic Squeeze and Madness music videos. Some gamble at slot machines, some sleep, some enterprising members of our touring party pick up booze and smokes at the duty-free shop, which doesn't open until we're in international waters and closes before we port. We can see the white cliffs of Dover in the distance as we approach the Kingdom. I will reference these cliffs in a song soon and refer to them as "peaks" in order to make the rhyme work. But these are cliffs, I am aware of that, I always have been.

We gather in the pub on the ferry and map out our plan like a bank heist. Everything goes in the van except backpacks. Action Rob, being English, can enter the country with cargo no problem. Braid will ride in the sedan pretending to be tourists. We will leave the ferry on foot as students abroad, "out on holiday from university," I find myself saying, fancying myself clever for using British lingo.

"What are you studying at university?" the immigration officer asks. Fuck. I wasn't prepared for that. In a panic, I find myself blurting out "Math" like Ralphie on Santa's lap in "A Christmas Story." I've lost all sense of myself, no idea if I pulled that off. "Alright," he says, and stamps my passport. I am shaking as we all make it through unscathed. I cannot believe that actually worked. I haven't slept a wink but I'm so keyed up that I'm wide-eyed all the way to London.

We end up at the promoter's flat and I am offered their bed. I sleep most of the day but it is fitful and restless sleep. Most day-after-night-drive sleeps are restless, dreams are more intense and sometimes I can't wake up. I become aware that I'm dreaming and try to pull myself out of it, but can't. It's only if I surrender that I can relax enough to end the visions.

I awake sometime in the afternoon, and we're off to a chippie for some authentic British grub. England doesn't feel that different from the States, I notice. That makes sense, I guess. It's older, but since our customs were based on theirs it's really not much of a culture shock. We're not so different in the colonies, are we?

The London gig is in the basement of a pub. We drink warm pints of ale and hang out with some friends who have flown over from New York. They are in the fashion industry, and even in their early twenties they travel for work a lot so they were able to write the trip off as a business expense. It's nice to see some familiar faces. The show is good, Braid takes top billing as they are more popular in the UK. They are on a hipper indie rock label over here, and what they lack in mainland distribution they more than make up for in English hype. I buy what I call a "Newsies" cap and Action Rob says I look like a "Geordie." I have no idea what that means. After the show, over pints, we're apparently chatting too loud and are told if we're "gohna toook, toook oootside," so we retire to the patio as the pub closes down.

Leeds is Action Rob's hometown and we are staying at his house. The pubs shut down at 11:00 p.m. I ask what folks do once they close, and Action Rob says "fight, mostly." We meet Action Rob's friend Andrew, who will henceforth be known as "Action Andrew" to all of us. He's gonna tag along with us for a few days. Great, we are already crammed on top of each other, what's one more bloke?

We stop for petrol, and when Action Andrew returns to the van he starts emptying out his pockets of all the food and beer he's stolen from the shop. He also wants to smash the state but lives on the dole. I can't help but feel that he's gonna get us in trouble somehow.

The guitarist in Braid was sleeping in the van, it being his night for guard duty, when he was awoken by young locals running across the roof. This is something they do here when they're done fighting for the night. The local street toughs play leapfrog over parked cars. Must have been a terrifying thing to wake up to.

Glasgow, Manchester, Liverpool, and then back down to Brighton, where we perform in the hull of a docked boat. Then it's up the coast back to Dover and across the Channel back to France. Action Andrew has forgotten his passport, so once we're on the boat we rearrange the gear to make a pocket between the amplifiers where he can hide. From Calais we drive to Brussels, where we're playing with an American hardcore band from Long Island called Cleanser. Their singer is good friends with The Collector. Small world. We play kicker into the night, getting our asses handed to us by the locals.

Amsterdam is beautiful. I feel sorry for any live music fans who go to see American bands here, as they all have to endure our enthusiasm for the abundance of legal drugs. We are playing a show with another American hardcore band called Battery. They are from DC, and they also know some people we do back home. They are avowedly straight edge, and somehow we're on the bill for what is advertised as a straight edge festival? That's news to us, we're stoned out of our gourds right now. I think it makes sense for youth who have grown up in a culture that is so open with its vices to rebel by not partaking, even boycotting them. Thus, a big straight edge scene in Amsterdam, who woulda thunk it?

After the show we are put up in a hostel. One room, ten bunks, shower down the hall. It's my night to sleep in the van, which has been parked on the street in front of a brothel. A woman who is as thick as a linebacker is barking "fifty guilders, suck or fuck" at the top of her lungs, attempting to lure would-be Johns. I walk to the kebab shop and grab a couple of beers. I'm a lightweight so this should put me right out. I drink myself to sleep on the van's middle bench seat holding a tire iron. Nobody's getting in here tonight.

Hamburg, more debauchery. We visit the club where The Beatles played, wander the streets of the Reeperbahn, including the men's only block. Prostitutes dressed like snow bunnies are calling out for dates. I walk by a window with a display of a dominatrix holding a leash attached to a large naked man wearing a zipper mask and masturbating. It's, uh, unique.

A friend from Kansas City who is on vacation here comes to our show. He's taken aback by the amount of activity in the crowd. People stage dive, crowd surf and circle pit at our shows in Germany. To them we seem to be a hardcore band so the usual hardcore show rules apply. That's not how it is for us in the States, at least not yet. Our friend joins in wholeheartedly, surfing his way to the stage to grab the mic and scream a chorus before diving face first into the masses.

I'm starting to get what I have come to call "cathedral fatigue." We've been on this continent for five weeks and I am about at my limit. I don't want to go see any more sights, I'm sick of kebabs, I'm definitely sick of room temperature meat and cheese on baguette. What I really want is a burger or a slice of pizza or The Bell. The Photographer mocks me, I'm younger than him but don't have the same stamina for wanderlust that he does. He'll go on to travel the world many times over and document the whole thing. I'll go on to travel the world over and see the inside of a van, then a club, then an apartment or hotel room. Rinse and repeat.

The last night in Germany is the last night of the tour. We are to walk offstage, load out and head straight to the airport. Action Rob is gonna drop us off and we'll have to either stay up the rest of the night or sleep on the floor until our early morning flight. He's gonna take the backline back to the creepy self-portrait guy after he drops us off. We're on last tonight and after we play we kick over all the drums, Nirvana style. We don't break anything but we really make it known that we are done and that we are ready to go home. Drenched in sweat we pose for a Polaroid in front of the stage. We're just babies, like when you see a picture of your grandfather in his military uniform. Old enough to know better, but young enough to pretend.

Once we get home we do the math, counting out our money after paying Action Rob, the backline, the merch, booking agent, petrol, tolls, fees, and other expenses. We've each netted two hundred bones for six weeks of work. That's actually more than I thought we would make. If we could break even and not lose any money I figured this would be worth it. All I want to do is tour, and Europe was really high on the list.

When I get back to my future in-laws' house my jet lag keeps me awake all night. It's the early days of email so I rattle off a few, confirming interviews or answering questions about the band. Remembering that Mr. Happy doesn't sleep, I whip out my phone card and make the long-distance connection to New York. He's got three weeks confirmed from here to the tip of Florida and back starting in a month. "Perfect," I tell him and let him off the line, retiring to my bed.

Honey White's younger sister has taken her room while big sis is at college. I've got a free place to stay in her childhood bedroom, which is painted a garish princess pink with white accents. It looks like a cupcake. I turn on the 13" television and VCR combo and watch *Twin Peaks* again for the umpteenth time. In an hour the house will be bustling with activity as my future family rises for work and school. They turn on every television in the house as they ready themselves for the day, leaving everything on when they depart.

When I finally wake up the first thing I do is walk through the house silencing the idiot boxes. Then it's quiet. I haven't been quiet for six weeks, I've been coexisting with upwards of twelve other men for the better part of two months. I should savor this, I think to myself. I pour myself a cup of very black, very bad coffee and wait for it all to sink in. The house is silent, I am alone with my thoughts for the first time since I can remember and it scares the ever living shit out of me.

Virgin Herb

I don't have any earthly idea who this band is. Mr. Happy set us up with our first proper opening slot, the first of three supporting what I'm told is a Christian pop-punk band called MxPx. I don't have a great history with either of these demographics so I am a little hesitant. Around the time that the Get Up Kids started I was also playing bass in a short-lived pop-punk band. My departure from pop punk to start a "fucking emo band" was met with much mockery. There was never any doubt which band I would choose, but once they told me I didn't look like a singer, more like a bass player (whatever that means), I bounced. Plus, there was the whole Catholic school experience that didn't really improve my attitude towards the devoted. I doubt they are gonna try to convert me, I'd like to see them try.

I've never been on a support tour before. We're about two years behind the wheel but all the basement and all-ages spaces we've played have been co-headline, though we don't call it that. We just call them shows, not concerts, not gigs, we don't even use the word "venue" yet. The word "show" is both the performance itself as well as the space that it happens in. I'm also reluctantly starting to use the word "merch" instead of just "shirts." The headliner has a lot of merch, a whole sidewalk sale's worth of designs. On more than one occasion I will see an adult purchase damn near one of everything because "you gotta support the Christian bands." God has deep pockets, I remind myself.

I don't know this scene at all, none of us do. It's apparently a pretty lucrative way to make a living. Our only real exposure to it is a kid we know back home who makes really nice drums with his dad. He grew up playing in bands like this. He tells us his band would play Christian music festivals and do crazy numbers at the merch table. This blows my mind. It's like learning for the first time there's more than one flavor of ice cream, it just never occurred to me that such a thing could exist.

We are at a bowling alley in Nebraska, first night of the tour. The drum-making kid is with us just for this one night, he's gotta see this for himself, his friends opening up for the musical manifestation of his former life. Sipping a now-discontinued cinnamon liqueur called After Shock, he asks us what we're gonna do if people ask us to sign Bibles. "We're not signing any fucking Bibles," one of us exclaims within earshot of the headliner. Our new hosts stare daggers at us. Great first impression, that.

This is also the first tour in the States without Amy. Our 1995 Ford Econoline with the wooden bumper has served us well but the radiator has given up the ghost, and besides, Cujo has us covered. Cujo is the comedian, our "vibe" tech we will come to call him. He keeps us from fighting as best as he can. He has a Dodge van with an extended top, complete with loft and, get this, a fucking TV/VCR and an original Nintendo. What are we, Aerosmith? This is gonna be a breeze.

It's nothing compared to the headliner's tour bus, but it's still the nicest ride we've ever had. One catch, Cujo is the only one who can drive it. This rule will be adjusted on nights he's drinking, when I'll take the wheel. Not Jesus, just me. In the meantime I'm gonna play video blackjack, or spread out on the loft that actually has enough room to kind of sit up a little bit. Not a lot, but it's still better than we've ever had.

We round out the crew with J-Bone, who is now tech-bubble poor after the crash. He just wants an excuse to leave town, depressed about his new financial situation. Just don't get too drunk to count money and don't leave anything behind, we tell him.

The shows are bigger than we're used to. Larger clubs, some theaters, still shitty green rooms, at least for us, but that's better than we've previously had. The headliner's tour manager is a rarity, a woman, and she is not to be fucked with. She reprimands Cujo for taking a bagel from their rider. It was just part of the spread in the communal dressing room, he didn't know it was off limits. She's gotta be tough though, women on the road, let alone tour managers, are unicorns. She needs to make sure all these pig-headed knuckle draggers know from moment one that she's the only motherfucker in charge. I am immediately impressed with her badassery, she doesn't give two shits about any of us.

I'm gathering that the headliner is going through something of a transition in their career. Not trying to deny their Christian roots, but not really trying to put it on front street either. This is a tricky thing to do. You'll never get true mainstream acceptance if you are just a "Christian band" but you also run the risk of angering and alienating your original fanbase who might assume you've "sold out," whatever that means. The headliner left their smaller Christian indie label where they had success and have made the leap to a major. Popular punk is hot right now, and this band is good and willing to do the work. They have a solid following and if the right label can find that sort of musical separation of church and state they could actually get pretty mainstream big. Radio big, maybe even stadium big. I don't know anything about any of that shit. We're just here to wipe the floor with their asses, nobody is gonna forget about the opener on this tour.

I play a 1972 Fender Tele Custom the color of a dark cigar. We don't call them "Custom Telecasters," just "Tele Custom," this is our common gear parlance. The exception is any Gibson Les Paul with a gold paint finish, which is simply a "Gold Top," no need for any other description. The only possible distinguisher is if it has "humbuckers" or "mini-buckers," denoting the size and sound of the pickups.

I've been in search of a Tele for a while and could only really find them in Texas, being the standard guitar for country pickers. They are out of vogue in the rock circuit, and punk kids certainly don't play them. Gibson is the flavor of guitar in our scene, SG mostly, that's what Jim plays. I fancy myself some sort of modern greaser, my hair slicked back with Royal Crown, wearing Levi's cuffed at the boot, western shirts or mechanic uniforms complete with a patch bearing another man's name. I think Teles look cool, and nobody I know plays them. I just hate the tiny headstock, it looks so silly, like a baby toy on the end of shotgun. The Tele Custom has a Stratocaster headstock which, unlike the rest of that particular guitar, looks cool as hell. I found this beautiful beast in Boston of all places, got a steal on it, too. Berkelee kids don't wanna look like Buck Owens, but I do.

After a show in Indiana we go to stay at the house of an older guy who is interested in managing us. He kinda reminds me of the guy my dad moved in with after my mom kicked him out, real Boomer energy. The house is huge, with the obligatory Woodstock print and a very clean, not often ridden Harley in the garage. This guy says he used to date Stevie Nicks and that he would blow cocaine up her ass when she deviated her septum from partying too hard. Even if this ridiculous story is true, TMI, bud. This is the first time we've hung out with a "music industry" person and I am less than impressed. I'll take the hospitality but we're not gonna be working with this joker anytime soon.

The gang has procured some marijuana and I decide to try it for the first time. We give each other comical weed names: Dank Nuggs, Bongzilla, Roach Dog, Sir Tokes A Lot and me...Virgin Herb. The experience, though mild, is not too dissimilar from having low blood sugar. I'm just, like, really...hungry. A bag of Doritos later, I curl up under the pool table and drift off to sleep.

The tour takes us to Louisville, and we're on our own turf. It was one of the first cities to embrace us and we've played here a lot. We have a crew in this town and a lot of our friends are working the show. We all laugh about how weird it is that we're on this tour. The club is usually for stripping and there is a catwalk down the front of the stage that leads into the audience. The headliners have wireless guitars and will take advantage of the strange extra stage space, but we are tethered to our amplifiers. After the show the young crowd takes longer than expected to buy merch and the club wants to reset for the dancers so they can make some actual money, as these kids don't buy booze. An old local hardcore scene legend named Rat, who looks like a moonshiner and had dumbfounded everyone earlier by making a racist joke about the mostly Asian main support band, opens a garden hose on the crowd to disburse them. He just spectacularly sucks, but I still laugh, I can't help myself.

In North Carolina we play an outdoor reggae bar, which is an odd choice of venue for this tour. We go on earlier than usual, and a group of kids who got tickets specifically to see us show up too late. They ask if we want to come back to a friend's art gallery and play for their crew. They'll buy us a case of beer for our trouble. We oblige, and upon arrival we learn that there is no PA at this gallery. We set up and some phone calls are made, but no speaker system can be procured. We decide to play anyway.

The crowd unites to sing every word with me as we play. It's like an electrified campfire sing-along, "Kumbaya" with a drum kit. Afterwards we follow the gallery owner to his house to crash. He lives with his dad out in the boonies and his father carves headstones. Their house looks like it's in the middle of a cemetery, the old man's talents spread out across their land. The inside of the house is carpeted everywhere, even the kitchen and bathroom. There are three small dogs jumping on us as we sleep, the whole place reeks of their urine.

In retrospect, these are the shows that are the most meaningful to me. The music industry milestones that we will eventually hit will never loom as large in my memory. Besides the general sense of community that one can only really achieve in compact spaces, small shows are generally more fun and certainly more interesting. This is why I started playing music, to finally be able to connect with people with common interests. It's something that can't be replicated en masse.

Fells Point, Baltimore. on Halloween. We are costumed, me in goth makeup, some of the others in drag. The Collector is here. The Sisters, too, having made the drive down from New York. At the end of the night someone is sitting on the toilet puking between their legs. J-Bone got so pissed he walked out to the van, vomited on himself, stripped down to his tighty whities and went to sleep in the loft. It turns out our merch was left behind but the headliner is going to bring it to the next show for us. They must think we are maniacs. This is one of the nights that Cujo lets me drive, me being the only sober one in the van. The Collector lets us crash at his extravagant dorm room for the final time. He's graduating next semester and moving back to the city. We're gonna have to find a new place to sleep in this part of the world.

We're going to Canada for the first time and are concerned about immigration and taxes we may have to pay on the items we intend to sell in their country. You can get away with calling a certain amount of it "promotional material," but not as much as we've got. We take a screwdriver and remove the back wooden panels of the speaker cabinets. We fill them with as many shirts as we can squeeze between the speaker cones and replace the panels. Same goes for the kick drum and our personal luggage. The whole process takes over an hour and now all our gear is incredibly heavy.

We pass from Vermont into Quebec Province with no problem. It's a small and out of the way border crossing and they don't even inspect the gear or ask for a manifest or anything. All that work for nothing, but you can bet your ass that if we hadn't done it we would have gotten searched and fined and screwed. That's just the way these things go.

The headlining band's manager is on their bus for the next couple of days, probably because we just played New York and he wants to network. He's got a weird energy, very LA manager mixed with youth pastor, and he uses so much industry slang it makes my stomach ache. He's also got an ex-addict-turned-religious-zealot vibe, which is probably good for him but I don't want to hang out with the dude. After the show in Trois-Rivières we're invited to DJ at a club. I think they expected us to play punk classics and songs by our contemporaries, but we spin exclusively Top 40 pop music of the past decade. The kids dance in spite of themselves. A good hook is, after all, a good hook, no matter how mainstream it is.

The next day word comes down that the manager douche caught one of our crew doing party drugs at the DJ set. He wants us kicked off the tour. I protest that we're just drunks, we don't do shit like that. I ask the accused party, who reassures me that he did no such thing, so I go to bat. I tell this judgmental prick manager that he didn't see what he thought he saw, and get both the headliner's tour manager and Mr. Happy to vouch for me. You trust me, right? I'm nothing if not a stand-up guy. If I say we didn't do that, then my word is bond. We are allowed to stay on the tour and the manager flies back to coke-fueled Los Angeles. I will come to find out years later that the accusation had been true all along. I had unknowingly lied on behalf of a guilty man. He will be unrepentant, I will be furious.

We finish the tour having left an impression on this world of popular punk. The headlining band were lovely to us, treated us like equals, but this scene is weird. It's more competitive than we're used to, but that will prove to be a template for our future. As our friends start getting famous it will prove hard not to become green with envy. But, for now, we are the Young Turks, the new blood, and we laid waste and left them wanting. Left them hungry for more.

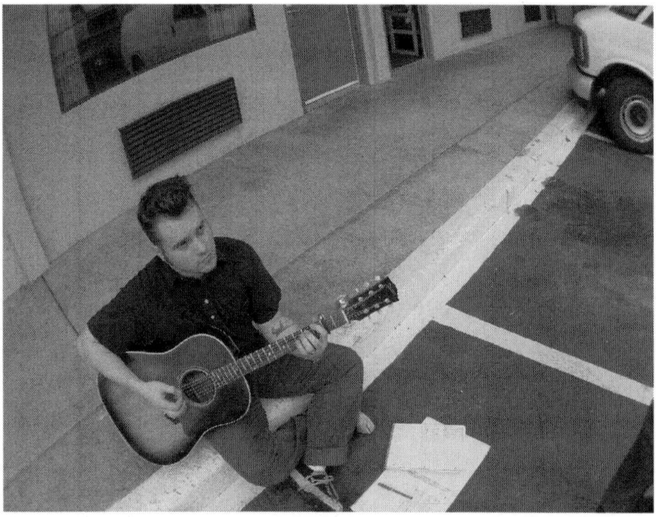

The Company Dime

James and I are driving around the city in his pink Geo Tracker listening to music and writing harmonies for songs that don't have any. Fuck, these songs are good but the shit we're writing would take them over the top. He's nursing a Rolling Rock and a dart as we make our way to the Hurricane, where his new girlfriend works. I wish he wouldn't drink and drive but it's his car, what am I gonna do about it? I also wish he didn't hang out with this girl, she's mean as a bag of snakes and he's a puppy dog. I guess he has a type.

Ever since he moved in with The Popes we've been hanging out a lot. He and I are the only ones in the group who are of legal drinking age and we have a shared bond over singing. At the piano in the dining room he has this uncanny ability to sound out and play any popular song you can throw at him. He is a remarkably talented piano player, and a pretty sick drummer, too. Plus he writes these hilarious original tunes that are actually really good. He delivers pizzas and so always has extra cash from his tips. He is the drunkard's ATM since I'm always broke and he wants someone to drink with.

He teaches me about music theory and how to sing harmonies. A good harmony should make the hairs on your arm stand up, he tells me. I know exactly what he's talking about, though I have no idea how to execute something like that. He teaches me about thirds and fifths, which are the most common harmonies in pop music, and I absorb it like a sponge. He invites me to come sing on Coalesce's Led Zeppelin cover record. I've got the highest male voice of anyone we know, and nobody else is gonna hit those opening notes of "Immigrant Song." In that session he harmonizes with me, and it turns out we sound pretty damn good together.

We've been kicking around the idea of adding keys into the mix and maybe he's the guy for the job. When we come back to the same studio where the "Immigrant Song" session happened to make our contractually obligated EP, we bring him along to play piano and sing. For one song in the session he arranges a string part and even writes it out on sheet music for the cellist who came in from the music program at the university. It turns out to be incredible. We need him to be in the band. The only problem is he's leaving for a tour with Coalesce, so if we are gonna work together it's gonna have to be down the line.

We hunt for a new partnership with a record label. The label we signed to has made it very clear that, even though we're on the uptick, it's his distribution company that is the priority. He can't print records fast enough to keep up with both our touring schedule and the distribution to stores. One of them has gotta go, and he's chosen us.

My blood boils over this. We are out on the road two-hundred-plus days a year and the only way we can make burrito and gas money is to sell merch. If we can't get records then we've got no music to sell. Sure, we can sling cotton, but the album is what we're promoting, not the shirt. So we are actively seeking a bigger label to work with, and we tell him that. He's fine with it because we're still under contract for a second record, which means he's gonna get paid either way.

Side note: A band / label partnership is just that, a partnership. It's a symbiotic relationship, one cannot exist without the other. Sure, if the band didn't make the music then there would be nothing to sell. But if there isn't a good label to sell it then that music is essentially in a vacuum. You can't get people to listen to something if they don't know it exists. Whenever one side or the other in this marriage starts to think that they are the only reason for their success, it's only a matter of time until the relationship falls apart. A good partnership, and I've had a few, is based on trust, hopefully respect as well. Keep that in mind and you'll both go far.

I have no love for the people I have met so far in the record industry. Aside from a mere two mensches who I will remain lifelong friends with, everyone else appears to be full of shit. We've met with several slightly-older-than-us white dudes who've told us how great we are and have taken us out to dinner on their corporate accounts. If that initial meeting goes well we'll eventually get to meet their boss, an older white man, sometimes with a white ponytail. This guy will invariably have an original Arnold Skolnick Woodstock poster on his wall and will tell us stories about the bands of the '60s and '70s. One of these types is the guy who used to date Stevie Nicks.

If the boss-level meeting goes well and we want to work with this label, then Our Manager can start talking terms. This is where, every time thus far, they fuck us. These charlatans who have repeatedly told us that we are God's new gift to pop culture won't even offer us enough coin to buy us out of our shit indie deal. Then why are we even talking? We can't legally work with you anyway. Did you think you'd just find a loophole in our stupid little indie label's contract that meant you could sign us for free? You obviously have no idea who The D Man's lawyer is. That guy represents every New York hardcore band around, he didn't get that rep for being an idiot or for being soft. Hell, I'm terrified of the guy. That contract is iron clad, that's the whole fucking problem. We want out, and the only possible way to do that is with fifty grand.

There are two exceptions to the rule that everyone in the industry is full of shit. One from Seattle and one from Arizona. The one from Seattle is a true believer, a pop historian, a real lover of music. He tries to sign us to Sub Pop, an indie rock institution, the kind where you might pick up a record from a band you've never heard of just because of that label on the back of the sleeve. I know I've done it. His boss offers us less money than we're getting from The D Man. I assume he thinks

their credibility is enough to win us over even with the pay
cut. The one from Arizona is also pure of heart and has a track
record. He's signed bands—granted, bands we don't like—that
have gone on to put out huge records. The label is called Mojo
and their track record of getting bands on the radio is
outstanding. They have one pop punk band, one ska band,
one swing band, and are apparently hoping for one emo band.
That's supposed to be us.

They have major label money and are willing to give us a proper
recording budget. We really believe in Arizona, he really gets us
and has the bona fides to take us to the next level. Again though,
the buyout is a non-starter. This negotiation goes on for
months. During that time I alternate between phone calls with
Our Manager and Arizona, desperate for any progress updates.
For six months we don't tour and we don't work day jobs. We
are positive that this will be resolved and we'll be getting our
advance any moment now.

We do write, a lot, often about these frustrations in our lives.
In a mostly abandoned building in a soon-to-be-gentrified
part of town, we occupy a third-floor office with no access to
a bathroom. We are young men, and young men are gross. We
fill the room with soda bottles of urine, dumping them into
the water fountain in the hall when the smell becomes toxic.
Eventually we will take to urinating directly into the water
fountain. I don't know if the other bands that practiced there
ever actually drank from that fountain. I shudder to think.

Eventually I am sneaked onto a conference call between
Our Manager, Arizona, the label's lawyer, The D Man and his
terrifying representative. I clutch my pearls at the amount
of vitriol and anger between these parties. There is no way
these stubborn bastards are going to hammer out this deal.
We decide to run a quick tour out West to make some money,
and to take a meeting with Our Manager and Mojo. It's James'
first trip with us. We've made him a half-member of the band,
whatever the fuck that means. I guess it means he does just as

much work but only gets half since he's new? It's a negotiation that seems to make sense at the time.

The shows out West are great, but the meeting is a disaster. These people obviously hate each other, especially Our Manager. It becomes painfully obvious that there is no way this relationship could work even if we can get bought out from The D Man, and that hasn't been agreed upon either. Arizona's label will advance the fifty grand but it's gonna have to come out of our recording budget, leaving us with next to nothing to make the record with. There is no point, in my opinion, to sign anything unless you're either getting paid or getting complete creative control. Here we are, getting neither.

Did I forget to mention they are demanding that we re-record a song from our first album? That's another thing we can't do anyway because of our old contract. We can't re-record anything for ten years, that's the term. This is the breaking point for me. If we're entering into a business relationship and you think my best work is behind me, then you do not have faith in the future of this partnership. And I, therefore, do not have faith in you.

We are fucked. The prospect of being stuck on the old label for even one more record makes me want to break the band up. Maybe we could start a new project with a different name and be free of it all. This, of course, wouldn't work. We'd all signed that contract as individuals, The D Man would have right of first refusal for all future projects. Still, part of me just wants to set the whole thing on fire, watch our hard work burn to the ground.

But then, from that fire, a phoenix. Our Manager suggests we release the record on his tiny independent record label called Vagrant. He'll find a way to come up with enough money to buy us out and still have a decent-sized recording budget. Sounds like a long shot. No indie label is going to let us leave to go to another, smaller indie label, right? He thinks they might if he can sweeten the deal, maybe give them the vinyl rights? Nobody gives a shit about vinyl these days anyway. Surely it's dead as disco. Plus, if we gamble on his company, what we'll lose in up-front cash we'll make up on the back end. We'd be investing in ourselves as much as him. Out of desperation, we decide to give it a shot.

We are writing, writing, writing. Demoing with a friend of James' named Lance Attack. This friend has an ancient multi-track recorder and doesn't really talk. He comes to our disgusting rehearsal space and helps us put some ideas to tape. I've got all my lyrics in a small Moleskin notebook that I keep in my backpack along with my insulin kit and syringes. One night, while we're rehearsing on the third floor, someone steals the bag out of the van. Even as furious as I am, I really hope they don't do anything stupid like use the insulin or the used syringes. That could kill a normal person. Regardless, the first drafts of my lyrics are gone. Luckily, some of them have been recorded and can be recovered, but some are lost to time. Probably lesser drafts anyway, I tell myself.

After recording the demos, we load everything into Amy the van and park it at the Valentine House. This is where The Popes and James reside. Where James plays the piano, and we all watch *Twin Peaks* and drink Rolling Rock whenever James comes home with pizza delivery money. He's found that if he wears a long wig and blasts hair metal from his pink Geo Tracker that he gets better tips from the dirtbags he delivers to. We are all wicked broke as we are foolishly waiting to sign a record deal and get a supposedly huge recording advance.

One day we're drinking coffee on the lawn, keeping an eye out for the tour bus Our Manager has sent to take us to California. Many bus companies are headquartered in Nashville to support the country music industry there. Sometimes if they aren't hired for a Nashville-based artist they have to deadhead to wherever an artist is starting their tour. "Deadhead" means a drive day, a day without a show. I will come to hate deadhead days, it means spending the entire day on the bus watching five dollar bin movies from Walmart. It would be awesome if I were a stoner who played video games. Alas, I am not.

We are not going on tour this time, but this bus is deadheading from Nashville to Los Angeles, which is where we are going to record. Our Manager got the bus for a song because it was passing through Kansas City anyway, and the bus company can make a few extra bucks by double dipping. The band this bus will be meeting in Los Angeles is still paying for the deadhead days, too. We meet the bus driver, he's a good ol' boy and makes a homophobic joke right off the bat. Glad he's in the cab and we're in the back.

The ride is smooth and we strategize about the record, "fantasize" is probably a better way to put it. We don't know the guy we're recording with from Adam. Our Manager hooked us up with him, and I think he's the reason we got a such a sweet deal on the studio we'll be working at. It's a world-class joint owned by a Scientologist. Welcome to Los Angeles, boys. Since we don't know this producer we bring along Wonder Kid, who has been doing front-of-house for us on the road. He at least knows what we want to sound like. Plus, I think he wants to produce records, too, so he's down for this *staj*.

We arrive at Toshi's place in Westwood. He works at the label and is really the reason we felt safe to sign there. He's younger than us but he gets it, we become fast friends. He lives with four other roommates who seem to have no idea why there is a tour bus in front of their modest ranch-style house. They also don't seem to have been informed that the six of us will be staying in their home for the coming weeks. Some of us are in the guest house out back, but most of us are on the couch or the floor in the main space. It's fine, we're spending most of our days at the studio and are not really gonna be here much anyway.

A week into our stay at Toshi's he fucks off and takes a last-minute gig doing merch on a pop punk tour. So now we're stuck with these four other roommates who we don't know at all, who didn't know we were coming, and who don't seem stoked that we're here. I take Toshi's bedroom, which turns out to be a godsend. After long days at the studio all the guys wanna do is get pissed and party. The cops get called several times, sometimes just because of us, we didn't even have people over. I hide away in Toshi's room and try my damnedest to tune them out so I can sleep.

Besides me getting his room, the other good part of Toshi's departure is that he's left us his car. It's a broke-ass I-don't-know-what clunker, but it will get the six of us across town to Silverlake and back every day. The traffic is brutal even though we're driving in the off hours.

The first couple of days we rent a rehearsal space to run through the songs for the producer and work out any last-minute ideas we have. When he shows up he's got a real industrial goth aesthetic, not our style at all. He sits in the corner and listens to a new song. We don't have a name for it but are calling it "Catfish" because sometimes James will play it on the Fender Rhodes in the style of an old blues man and sing the melody about fishing. This is obviously not going to be the final name or tone of the song. The producer takes some notes but doesn't talk much. He leaves saying he'll see us tomorrow at the studio.

Before we go to the studio the next day, we stop by the label offices and pick up our per diems, our day-to-day walking around money. The other co-owner of the label is the one who handles the cash and he does not like parting with it. He reluctantly hands us the envelope and we sign a receipt. We then immediately walk across the hall to Our Manager's office to play dice. After Our Manager takes a good portion of our money, if not all of it, we'll go back to the original office to ask for more so we can eat. He yells at Our Manager to no avail. They yell at each other a lot. Afterwards we go to a strip club for lunch, literally just for lunch, as they offer a buffet and we're living on a few dollars a day.

This studio is gorgeous, it's got a grand piano signed by one of The Beatles. We're gonna track drums and piano in the spacious A room but everything else in the much smaller, and therefore more affordable, B room. When it comes time to do the vocals we cover the window between the isolation booth and the control room. The studio has a curtain for just such an occasion. We're not the first band to get stage fright singing in front of a room of judgmental peers. James and I procure some whiskey to drink while doing the vocals to loosen up. We get a little too loose, he starts making animal noises instead of vocal harmonies. Somebody else is gonna have to drive Toshi's shitbox back to the house. I'm too in the bag.

We're in a part of town that is about to get very hip but for now our only options for food are a shitty pizza place and a shitty taco stand. There is a grocery store nearby but we don't have a way to cook anything at the studio so that's kind of a bust. The industrial goth producer is turning out to be a pretty good hang, he's not trying to Reznor-ize our songs and he's getting good sounds and has good ideas. There's an old timer, Dale, who works at the studio. He's kind of our liaison with the property. For "Out of Reach," the one song with a prominent acoustic guitar, I've restrung the 1960 Gibson I bought from my soon-to-be father-in-law and the new strings sound bright and tinny, like a new country album. Dale brings in an old Martin with strings that haven't been changed in decades. It's kind of a bitch to play but it sounds amazing on the track.

Before recording the piano on "I'll Catch You," James walks directly into one of the sliding glass doors on his way to the Steinway grand. He's bleeding on the keys but gets the take before he has to lie down on the couch. We've borrowed some amps from a friend and we layer guitars a ridiculous number of times. I become deadly serious about the whole affair, analyzing every detail, stressing over every note.

I don't like this about myself, it's very stressful. I find myself getting irritated with my coworkers when they don't take the "job" as seriously as I do. I don't think it's a "job" to them, really, but it is to me. I know that we are making something better than we ever have before. All I can say is that I really like it, I'm proud of it. If logic stands, based on what's happened so far, if I like it, if we like it, the world is gonna fucking love this record. Mr. Happy comes to town and I play him some rough mixes in his rental car. "This is pretty good," he says as he nods. This is the most complimentary thing he's ever said to me, before or since.

We finally finish recording, and mixing is almost complete. We move out of Toshi's house and into a downtown motel that looks like the kind of places Tom Waits lived in when he moved to town in the '70s. Our girlfriends have flown out and we're gonna play a festival. The stage is erected out in a field, it's one of those bifurcated deals where the band on stage left is setting up while the band on stage right is playing. This is a cost-effective method for the promoter but it's a pain for the bands. It's hard to listen to another band do sound check and play your own song at the same time.

Some of our heroes are here, some cool actors, too. We get day drunk on trailer beers and all turn beet red from sunburn. This is a fitting way to end this adventure. Tomorrow we will fly home and wait for the world to change.

We don't have any artwork and we need some fast. We really should have thought about this more ahead of time. The record is going to come out in three months, we need album art. Jim came up with the title, *Something To Write Home About*, something his mom had said on the phone.

An older friend of Jim and The Popes who is named Travis but goes by Fudge is an artist. Fudge meets up with us at the Hurricane with drawings of robots. What the fuck do robots have to do with anything? The songs, the lyrics, the album title, none of them indicate robots. Fine, fuck it, there's no time to debate it, we need to get this turned in. The painting we choose for the cover is professionally photographed and sent to the label.

I have come to find out two unsettling things about our new business partners. One is that, in order to sign us, one of them had asked his parents for a loan. In order to produce this loan they have taken out a bank loan using their house as collateral. I don't want that kind of pressure. If this record tanks, I don't want to be responsible for some kindly old Jewish couple losing their home. The other unsettling thing is that they've gone into business with a manufacturer of pornography to make the CDs. This isn't inherently bad, but he's apparently now gone missing, presumed assassinated by the Chinese mafia. I guess this means we are one step removed from The Triads. Yikes.

Our Manager wants us to take a bus on the upcoming tour that coincides with the release of the album. He thinks the ambitious "anywhere and everywhere" tour I've routed is too long and has too many night drives to be safe. We've taken basically a year off from the road as we waited to sign a record deal and then made the record. This is an eternity, we're used to being gone two-hundred-plus days in a year. This break from performing leads me to assemble the most ambitious trip we've ever attempted, sixty-five shows in seventy days.

The tour will be broken into three legs. The first two weeks will start in a van with a trailer since we'll be out East and the drives are short. We won't have to drive at night much. The second and third legs will be on a bus. I don't know how to rent a tour bus, why the fuck would I know how to do that? Our Manager says he's on it. He works with a bigger band who have been using buses for a while now. We enlist Lance Attack to sell merch. He is not good at merch. We set off on the twenty-hour drive to New York.

Over the course of the three months between when we finished recording and started touring the album we've been busy on the backside. Part of our new record deal is that we got to start our own imprint label, so we've signed our friend's band, The Anniversary, from back home and James' silly side project called Reggie and The Full Effect. We've put together a showcase at CMJ and both of them are going to open for us.

We decided to be Reggie's backup band for this show, so we are playing a warm-up at a church in Philly. Surprisingly, there are no fights, a rarity for this town. After the show we randomly run into the comedian Sinbad at a Wawa and take Polaroids holding large bags of chips.

Mr. Happy has commissioned a printmaker to make posters for the show in New York featuring Evil Knievel. Did I mention he's obsessed with Evil Knievel? He has two photographs on the walls of his apartment: one of him with a young Mike Tyson, and another, larger one of him and Evil Knievel. I've only been in his apartment once. I spent the night there and he kicked me off the couch first thing in the morning because he had to go to work. "You work from home," I protested to no avail. He has an air conditioner but he never turns it on, even in the sweltering New York summer heat. I think this is to keep him mean, depriving himself of comforts like a warrior monk. Glad he's on our team.

The opening band on the rest of the tour consists of three Alabama hillbillies and one Connecticut Yankee called Hot Rod Circuit. We bond over a love of bands that increasingly fewer and fewer of our fans seem to have heard of. The Yankee becomes our drinking buddy, the hillbillies just smoke weed all day. They are a fun bunch, their songs are good, too. I think this first leg will be fun.

From here on out it's just "keep your eyes on the road." There is no plan *per se*, only a seeming compulsion to keep moving. If nobody hears these songs it won't be for a lack of trying. It's not wanderlust, we don't actually really see the places we go. It's more work lust, I guess they call that workaholism.

I am of a singular focus. We've been through too much bullshit the last year, and that's never gonna happen again. By the time this tour is ending, and we've gone back to where it started over two months later, things will be different. Not so different that it seems out of place, the shows are just bigger. I assume that's due to our hard work, and it is. We wrote the songs, we played the shows. But it would never have been possible without that little label that we decided to sign to as a last resort in a time of desperation. They work as hard as we do, making decisions I don't understand, and people are starting to notice.

Land Yacht

I am nursing a pint at The Replay Lounge, waiting for my life to change. I'm looking out for a guy named Tony. He will soon become known as "Crazy Tony," but as of now he's just some random redneck who is meeting me at the corner of 10th & Mass. A forty-five-foot-long 1983 Eagle pulls up and parks next to the bar. Tony, the driver, emerges and I greet him warmly. I offer to buy him a beer, but instead he wants to go across the street to the record store that doubles as a head shop. He needs to buy a bong. Nothing inherently wrong with that, but it is a memorable first impression. Crazy Tony is nothing if not memorable.

We are embarking on our most ambitious tour yet, the sixty-five shows in seventy days, the one for which our manager convinced us to get the bus as a matter of safety, saying that if we did that many night drives in a row in a van we would surely perish. I want us to play anywhere and everywhere that will have us, all the backwaters. The places where nobody goes are often the best shows because people are so grateful. Having grown up in a flyover state, I appreciate them as much as they do us. The bus is a matter of necessity because of the length of the tour, the tour is so long because of the expense of the bus. A snake eating its own tail of our own design.

Thing is, a bus is only as safe as its driver, and this dude is a psychopath. Initially his eccentricities are charming, but the looming knowledge that he holds our lives in his hands when behind the wheel is terrifying. A friend's band just rolled their van on a night drive and destroyed the guitar player's jaw.

Another band hit black ice and the drummer died in the crash. There are hazards, but this rolling deathtrap isn't safer, it's just bigger. It's the same logic as getting your kid an old, massive tank for a first car knowing full well they will wreck it, but at least they probably won't get killed in the crash. Safety or not, for the next two months, this rolling coffin is our home.

Day one, Our Manager yells at the tour manager—who isn't really a tour manager, he's a box truck driver we met on the support tour last year—for one thing or another. The tour manager takes it out on our merch guy—who isn't really a merch guy, he's the singer in a band we're friends with—for one reason or another, and now our cotton slinger is in tears. Meanwhile, we're in a bus at a VFW Hall in Sioux Falls, South Dakota. To some, this is a sort of treason. We suffer from a strange delusion in this scene. One is expected to suffer for one's art.

That sounds high minded, but let me explain. In this moment, there are rules, and we are breaking every one of them. Everyone has a right to make a living. It's not realistic to expect someone to keep losing money on a venture and continue to pursue it. That's what billionaires do to avoid paying taxes. The bus is a symbol of making your own comfort and supposed safety a priority. But, whatever, we're paying for the fucking thing. Just because one excellent band from DC took a vow of poverty doesn't mean we all have to adhere to that principle.

The show is good, if a bit small. That's fine, we are in South Dakota. Not exactly one of our "A" markets. I'm certainly guilty of being judgmental in the past of bands in buses that play small shows. Feels gratuitous somehow. Those bands, nine times out of ten, have tour support. We don't have the option of tour support. Our record label is beyond small and they barely got the money together to get us into the studio. But, for us, on this long of a tour a small show is fine. We've got some big shows on the coasts that will make up for this expense. We're getting to go where bands don't usually go, and that is the point.

We head north to Manitoba, where we've got a show that night in Winnipeg. The plan is to play two shows on the way west to Vancouver. We are rejected at the border. Well, we're allowed to enter the country, but something about tariffs on our merch makes it prohibitively expensive. Seems whatever country in Asia that manufactured the blanks we printed our name on doesn't vibe well with the Canadian government, so we can either pay a tax that is more than we will make at the gig, or we can turn around. We decide to turn around. I've still never been to Winnipeg.

We opt to spend the next two days deadheading to Seattle. In the back lounge we are thrown around like we're in a child's birthday party bounce castle. This feels inherently wrong, but we've never been on a tour bus before, I guess this is how it handles. In the middle of the night, somewhere in Montana, we are pulled over by a highway patrolman. He cites Crazy Tony with doing ninety-six miles per hour in a seventy zone. We should have fired him then and there. It's custom if your bus driver is a lunatic or a drunk or a racist or whatever that you call the bus company and have them send out a more suitable candidate, but we don't know that yet. Our Manager knows this, but he also co-owns our record label and is preoccupied with having to scramble to keep up with demand for our album.

Starting in Seattle and then making our way down Interstate 5, we set up shop and perform at all the venues that have rarely or never had a bus outside. It's not uncommon to double park the beast in front of a venue, drop the gear at record speed, and then move the bus off site. This has the added benefit of keeping our lavish death trap hidden from the eyes of would-be scenesters, the taste makers of the punk underground. We are rapidly approaching "I only like their early records" status. If they see the bus they will surely assume that this independent band with an independent booking agent on a tiny independent label has obviously sold out. That most cardinal of sins, its criteria ever changing depending on who and when you ask. No matter, we're here to work regardless of any naysayers.

It's in San Francisco that we first meet At The Drive-In. They are one of the most dynamic live music outfits I've ever seen and they are opening for us. Well shit, they're gonna eat our lunch. It's the indie rock equivalent of Jerry Lee Lewis setting his piano on fire before Chuck Berry and then daring him to top it. These motherfuckers are gonna be main support on the whole third leg of the tour, we're gonna have to up our game. One of them asks me if I wanna watch him jerk off in the park next to the club. I'm pretty sure he's testing me, seeing if I'm cool. The other asks me about our narcotic intake. I don't know that we're into that, just booze and weed, I tell him, pleased in my own ignorance. I'd really rather not know about it.

There's a movie star at the San Francisco show and she's hanging out with our merch guy. He is a wonderfully strange person, his uniqueness draws people in. It's hard to quantify. In Los Angeles, he won't walk onto the stage at The Troubadour, stating that he won't cross those hallowed boards until it's with his own band. I respect that, this place is sacred to me, too. The club is legendary, especially for a teenage metalhead like myself.

We do not have bad shows at The Troubadour. I made that decision the first time that we played there, when I leapt off the drum riser with a spin like David Lee Roth, and got to revel in the ability to do needle drugs in the bathroom like so many bands before me—though they weren't taking insulin. It's one of the only places I will give a pre-game speech. I don't give two flying fucks if your dog just died and you've been day drinking since before sound check, we DO NOT have bad shows at The Troubadour. Before it was gone CBGB's was the same, though there was nowhere private enough to give such a speech, not that it was ever necessary. Some venues are just too important to our past and our present, and sometimes our future. Best to treat them as such.

Honey White comes out to the shows in Los Angeles. She's still got another year of university in Boston but could use the break. We finagle the somehow-more-difficult-than-in-the-back-seat-of-a-car maneuver of coitus in my bunk. The bus shakes back and forth, not due to our passionate lovemaking but to an earthquake hitting at this most intimate of moments. It's like trying to fuck on a water bed, something we've accomplished but don't prefer.

She's only in town for the day but as always she's here to get down. The rest of the guys enjoy my company significantly more when she's around. It's not that she's oblivious to my personal hell of going to a bar after a show filled with said show's patrons, she just doesn't give a shit. My discomfort is the price for her good night out. I'll tolerate any piss-drunk punisher who wants to talk about the E-word over the house DJ, as long as she gets to dance. She would do the same for me.

The venue in San Diego is a punk collective close to, or maybe on, the university campus called "Che Cafe." The "stage" is made of milk crates topped with three-quarter-inch plywood, the PA is vocals only, and we have to park the bus right in front of the "venue." A contingent of the audience is visibly dismayed by our whip. They hurl coins at us as we perform. James is excited, more money for smokes. He proclaims from the stage, "Could you chuck something more productive, like cigarettes or a cold beer?" His request is not obliged. You know what? Fuck these college kids, I wanna go to Mexico.

After the show I take a road trip with Our Manager and his assistant to Tijuana. It's a short drive and an easy border for three gringos to cross. We belly up at an authentic-looking taqueria and I learn that Our Manager speaks impressively fluent Spanish. Apparently, most Los Angeles natives have at least a passable knowledge of the language. Growing up in Kansas City I've only got a passing understanding of how to speak hillbilly. Our Manager doesn't drink, he just decided not to one day in his youth. I have a margarita, as does his assistant.

It is a welcome respite, these times I can have a quiet conversation with Our Manager. He's a strategist, an idea man. We are the boots on the ground. He is becoming a father figure to me, my biological one not estranged but very distant.

I tease him about his supposed wife and kids who I've never met, insisting they don't actually exist. He assures me that they absolutely do, his pending divorce proof of their existence.

A mariachi band bellows narcocorridos and we talk about the coming year. Japan, Australia, back to Europe. He makes no mention of the potential collapse of the empire, the record label teetering on a razor's edge. Any misstep could send it into the abyss. I am grateful to be ignorant of this. It would have given me panic attacks.

I can't go to sleep. I don't trust Tony, he's becoming increasingly erratic. He was going on and on about seeing Jackalopes as we crossed the Arizona desert. I take to spending time by his side in the cab of the bus listening to his stories, nursing a drink until either exhaustion or alcohol pulls me under. I'm honestly scared shitless that he's going to kill all of us in some spectacular car wreck. I drink enough to get to the attitude of "if I wake up, I wake up" that I will later have to apply on planes after my daughter is born.

For now it's just me, the wine, and Tony's tall tales. He took a deep fryer onto a pontoon boat. The idea was to flash-fry fish they had caught right out of the lake. He drunkenly threw a full can of Pabst into the boiling oil and the whole thing exploded. He showed me the scar. Now I really can't sleep. This lunatic is the captain of this houseboat and I am certain we're all gonna die.

Texas goes well, same shady Sixth Street bullshit in Austin. No ticket count, only a house staff door clicker at the front, an easy way to rip off bands who just have a door deal. In Denton at Rubber Gloves, north of Dallas, we play a bunker next to a railroad track. The train is louder than the bands. Our sound engineer turns on the vocal-only PA and says, "There you go, I'm done with work, gonna go get drunk." Great.

From there it's north up I-35 and a day off at home. I stay on the bus, I don't have a home. Back on I-35, north to Minneapolis. I guess Prince owns this club? There is a lot of purple. It's

Halloween and we all dress up, Rob in drag as usual. At The Drive-In are on the tour proper but they don't don costumes. Their songs are too serious, they say.

In Pittsburgh I take a cab to get my grandmother's engagement ring resized. I'm gonna ask for Honey White's hand. We are just kids, but we both know it's been coming for a while. We've been together for the better part of eight years and survived four years of a long-distance relationship. My proposal won't be a surprise. I just hope she doesn't refuse me because of logic. We've still got a lot of living to do, and I hope that we can do it together, but I could see how one could be hesitant about marrying this young.

I cannot, for the life of me, get a cab back to the club. As it happens, one of the opening bands, Ultimate Fake Book, our friends from back home, are driving in the area because they are totally lost. I flag them down and climb into the back of their van. At the very least I know how to get back to the club.

A couple notable things about the show in Pittsburgh at Club Laga. One, the monitors are under the stage, behind metal grates beneath my feet. Never seen that before or since, it's ridiculous, a dropped pick is gone forever. The local opener plays one of our songs in their set and has a merch girl who will flash anyone who buys a shirt. Gross, to both. Then, a couple hours before bus call, Tony shows up to the show drunk. He starts yelling "Show me your tits!" to the mostly teenage audience. Our friends do the neighborly thing and escort him out. I'm regaled with stories the next day of Tony attempting to hire a prostitute, not knowing if they would be in the yellow pages under "H" for hooker or "W" for whore.

The next sign of trouble is in Philadelphia. Every time we play in Philly there is a fistfight. These same Neanderthals who used to call us pussies now seem all too happy to wreak havoc at our gigs. This one's in the basement of a church, the kind of place that would normally have twelve-step meetings. In the kitchen which doubles as a green room there's even a large percolator. A fight breaks out mid set, drawing all attention away from the stage. We stop playing. We're not going to be the soundtrack for this dipshittery.

The offending parties are ejected and the show resumes. Since everyone working security has decided to leave their post to watch us play, no one notices that one of the ejected parties has returned with reinforcements. This new mob begins to retaliate against the security who originally pushed them out. There is blood, much blood, ambulances are called. It's a bad, bad scene.

We head south, down Interstate 95. I loathe this highway, it can take four hours to drive a hundred miles on it. Madness. Richmond, Virginia, capital of the seceded South but traditionally a good turnout for us. This club holds about three hundred people, and about six hundred people show up. We can't do two shows. This tour is ten weeks long, if I double-gig it I'll blow out my voice for sure. First come, first served, and that usually means the younger, newer fans. The old guard, more accustomed to just showing up to their local and having a pint and a mosh, will have to miss out.

The local toughs don't like this young crowd. I don't totally get these kids either, but I don't have anything against them. We've slowly seen an evolution in the audience from our peers to their younger siblings. Not being able to emotionally relate to your audience still means you have an audience. Didn't Zappa say something about the industry being controlled by fourteen year olds anyway?

The bullies take over. They climb on stage and dive onto the unsuspecting newbies, punishing them for their inexperience. As if they had shown up at their first shows fully formed and aware of the rules. Everyone needs some band to be their gateway drug into punk rock, and that's us for these kids. The same meatheads who called us pussies are now claiming ownership of our band? Fuck that, first strike, we're gonna play nothing but ballads. Try to fight people to that. This is the south, turns out they can fight to anything.

Second option, we just stop playing outright. Unfortunately this punishes those who've already been punished, but we're not gonna play this game. They attempt to get physical, we decline. Little do they know that behind the mild-mannered glasses of The Popes there be dragons. They are lucky we depart. A handful of cars follow the bus out of town, hurling projectiles at us as we drive. We crank up the Zeppelin, spark a joint and crack a beer as we watch these fools in their pointless errand. "That'll show them," I assume they are reassuring each other, on the wrong side of history just like their forefathers.

Tony drives on the back roads, the ones too small for a vehicle this size. It's a miracle we don't get stuck driving under a bridge, but I do prefer the scenery. Predictably we are pulled over. Tony tries to convince the officer that we are playing the policeman's ball that night, so we need to be on these roads to get to the venue. The officer looks puzzled. He writes a pretty substantial ticket for the infraction and informs Tony that the interstate is a mile up the way and he better fucking get on it. This is his only warning. Hell, in fact he's gonna follow us all the way there. The band's first police escort, we've finally made it.

Turns out Tony wants to take the back ways because he doesn't want to pay the tolls on the interstate. He doesn't seem to grasp that we pay for the tolls, not him. We're probably going to have to pay for that stupid ticket, too. It will just get billed back to us by the bus company. Every couple of days the tour manager gives Tony a wad of cash called a "float." This is to cover tolls, gas, Tony's per diem and cab rides to and from his hotel room. He's the only one who gets a hotel room, and they aren't great. If I was driving a band and they put me up in one of those cockroach-infested abortion clinics I would be pissed.

New Jersey, Elks Lodge. The kids can't drink in the bar, but we can. We are honorary members here, having donated a portion of the last gig's door to flood relief in the area. They've even got our name on a plaque. These old timers love us, good Midwestern boys can hold their own with blue collar types. Everyone out here thinks we're bumpkins anyway.

Drinking with old timers is one of the great joys of life. You can simultaneously talk about the whole of the universe and nothing at all. It's so much more interesting than any bar in the city. Thank Christ we can hide out in this bar, too. These Jersey kids are kind of intense.

Back on the island at the center of the universe, we play Bowery Ballroom. Honey White comes down from Boston, she knows what's about to happen. The band walks onto the stage, and before I join them I pull her aside on the stairs and ask her to spend eternity with me. She accepts. I don't even remember the show. I'm told we played well, but I was on a cloud. We spend the evening together in a Days Inn across the river in Secaucus. You can't park a tour bus in the city, this is the closest spot. We'll get Denny's in the morning. I'm such a romantic.

I can feel my voice starting to weaken. We are sixty days into this tour with almost no days off and it's starting to take its toll. The madness is starting to set in, every day a roller coaster that repeats. Wake up, load in, do sound check, get dinner, clock in (start drinking), gig, tear down, load out, go out or go to bed. Rinse and repeat, day after day. I've found that I can't accompany anyone to a second location after the performance. I need to rest my voice back at the bus, where I'm often alone and always aware of when last call is, when the madness will come home to roost and I better be in bed with earplugs before it does. It's hard to be around drunks when you're trying to be quiet. I would love to be part of the fun but I've had an ache in my neck for a couple days now. Probably should get it looked at.

A "Rock Doc" is a physician who specializes in dealing with musicians, or at the very least will admit you last minute. Those who specialize in this particular aspect of the counterculture can often be called on for pharmaceutical favors. I know one guy in Philly who will trade homemade LSD just for guest list spots. I guess people just want to be part of the life however they can.

This one, in Cleveland, is pretty straight laced, happy that I don't smoke or do drugs, not crazy that I drink as much as I do. He sticks a long tube with a camera on it inside my word hole and makes a home movie. My vocal nodes are inflamed, very inflamed. He prescribes rest, no singing, little talking, and lots of water. Well, the first and second ones ain't gonna fuckin' happen, Doc. We've still got a week of shows left.

He offers me a shot of steroids right in my throat. Nope. We'll have to settle on the pill 'roids. They take a little longer to kick in, about twenty-four hours. We cancel the gig that night, the first time we've ever done that. This is the first time this has ever happened to me, I proclaim impotently. I feel not fear but anger. This is an inconvenience, and it's my fault. It is, of course, not my fault. It is normal strain on one's voice, but I still blame myself.

The next night we are in Detroit. It is, by far, the biggest show of the tour. The Majestic has four rooms: a small venue, a theater-sized venue, a restaurant and a bowling alley. We were booked in the small venue, the Magic Stick, but it sold out so fast we graduated to the theater. There are over a thousand people here to see us perform and I don't know if I will be able to sing. I haven't spoken in twenty-four hours. I give a few yelps into the microphone at sound check but don't sing a whole song. It's promising but not enough to prop up my confidence. I am, in a word, terrified.

This is the first time I become aware of the character I play. Backstage I'm a nervous wreck but silently carry on like nothing is wrong. I don't want my bandmates to feel the fear that I'm feeling. It's a moot point since they are oblivious to me, but that's where my mind goes. My heart is racing as we walk onstage. I put on my guitar, plant my feet, and become a different person. One who is confident, fearless, invincible. This is a lie.

For the next hour I live in perpetual fear of my voice failing me. It has come to be my kryptonite, the one thing that can stop me. Tonight the character I play prevails. I sing the notes I need to sing. For one number I ask the crowd to sing along and the whole room erupts with a chorus of voices that almost brings me to tears. They do not know of my fear, but they have vanquished it. Tell you what though, I'm never doing a fucking tour that long again, you can take that to the bank.

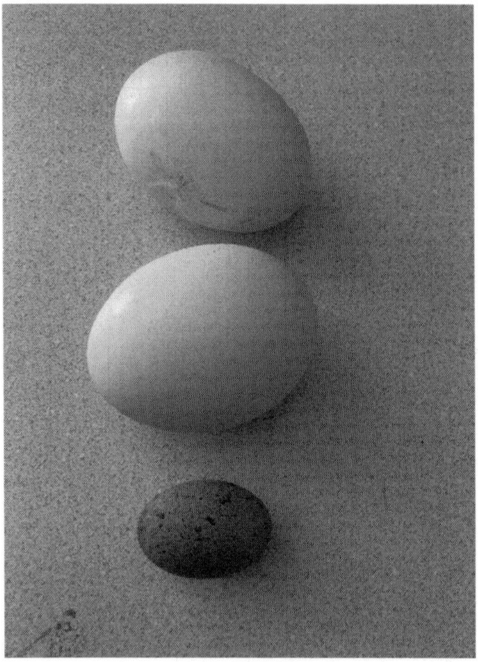

Sustenance

I am striding at a foolishly quick pace down ice-covered Commonwealth Avenue with an ostrich egg huddled under my peacoat. Nor'easter season in Boston is not to be trifled with, but I have braved the New England winter wind to procure this flightless bird's unfertilized offspring. Upon my return I immediately turn to our humble kitchen and attempt to crack the behemoth oval on the counter. It does not break, it does not even crack.

Ostrich eggs are the coconuts of breakfast foods, and I will spend the next half hour using knife, hammer and saw in an attempt to break into the cursed thing. I have done so much damage to the savory contents inside that I've rendered it inedible. How did I get here? Why have I braved frostbite and hypothermia just to acquire this exotic ingredient? One day they will label me a "foodie." The worst kind, one with a lot of disposable income to buy bullshit like this.

When the "anywhere and everywhere" tour is over, everyone goes home, but I still have more journeying to do. I wait a day, crashing on couches just to make sure everything gets put in its place, and then fly to Boston. I share a tiny apartment in the Allston neighborhood with Honey White and Our Mutual Best Friend. The apartment doesn't allow pets but I have inherited a cat named "Kitty" from James in a roundabout way.

Honey White being a full-time student, and Our Mutual Best Friend having a full-time job, I am alone most of the day. I often walk ten, fifteen miles a day listening to music on a Sony

Discman, getting lost in the maze-like neighborhoods of the city. It's cold here, and not just the weather, the residents are hardened. Probably callous from years of seemingly Arctic winters. It's a beautiful place, though. If you've gotta wander a city all day you could do worse.

I've taken to watching the Food Network when I'm not exploring. I am drawn in by how different it is from my life of touring. There are no carpeted stages, the floors sticky with old beer like walking through thick, wet sand. There are no green rooms covered in graffiti, band names and penises adorning all four walls. There are no truck stop burritos, no driving at all, and certainly no sleeping on the floor of a stranger's living room. What is this magical, sanitary, practical world?

I start scheduling my walkabouts around when my favorite of these programs, *Good Eats*, is on, never missing Alton Brown, the nerd who talks about science and history as much as technique. It was just this past Thanksgiving that we had the "turkey's too big" incident, attempting to roast one half of the bird at a time with the oven open. We did keep the windows raised. Honey White loves Sylvia Plath, but not that much. We could have just broken it down and roasted it on a sheet pan. I did not know this, I'm am not a good cook yet.

After my diabetic coma, food became utilitarian. Everything I ate had to be regulated and counted. It took all the joy out of eating. My mom was a fine enough cook, we ate middle-class Catholic fare. Braunschweiger on saltines, fried chicken livers, fish on Friday during Lent, turkey on Thanksgiving, corned beef and cabbage on St. Pat's. Back in her drinking days she would make green pancakes to go with her green breakfast beer on that most American of Irish holidays.

At school I would go to the nurse during the first part of my lunch break to give myself insulin shots, and then hurry back to inhale my meal in the little amount of time left. When I first moved out, I lived on instant ramen and discount blue box mac and cheese. When I started touring I ate almost exclusively

Taco Bell, pizza next door to the club, or whatever (usually vegan) nonsense the homeowner of that night's basement gig would make for us. Food was not a priority, it was just sustenance.

I doubt I've ever cooked anything more complicated than instant ramen for myself, but I am beginning to experiment. The band is doing well, and I have more money than I really know what to do with. I purchase and ruin expensive cuts of meat, blacken vegetables and burn rice, but eventually I get better. This becomes my other pastime while I wait for my roommates to return and soon I am cooking us dinner every evening. I also try to get them to watch the food shows with me but they want to watch wrestling. That's fine, I like wrestling, too.

Honey White gets me to try sushi for the first time, and oysters, too. I am very interested in their supposed aphrodisiac properties. I walk to "Stah Mahket" and get salt pork and clams to make "chowdah." French onion soup, roast chicken, steak and everything else from that first season of *Good Eats*. This guy in a bowling shirt is my Julia Child and I attempt it all.

When Honey White and I go back to Kansas City for the holidays we stay with her parents, and I start cooking for the whole family. That is, once I can find the kitchen. My future in-laws and their tween daughter have developed the nasty habit of doing the dishes weekly it seems. It's gonna take me over an hour to scrub these fucking pots and plates before I can even start to prep any food, let alone cook anything. I make them coq au vin, easily the most complicated and fanciest-sounding dish I've been wanting to try. I make a red sauce for pasta using cheap port. Turns out the port has a decent amount of sugar, which can take some of the edge off the tomatoes, plus the booze don't hurt.

My future mother-in-law's favorite meal is pork chops with mashed potatoes and corn on the cob. I brine double-thick chops and grill them and the corn in the husk, being sure to get perfect cross sections on the pork. I roast a bulb of garlic and combine the cloves, heavy cream and good butter into the potatoes as I mash them. I make sure everything is salted well. This does not matter, as my soon-to-be mother-in-law instinctively pre-salts her food before eating it. This drives me mad. At least taste it first, for fuck's sake.

Since the band has upgraded to a bus on the road, I start taking advantage of the satellite television to watch my food stories after shows. Since I don't go out post-gig to save my voice, I usually have the bus all to myself for at least an hour or two. Our current driver laughs at me, stating he's seen Christian bands get more pussy than us. This is the same guy who puts egg shells in his coffee grounds to cut back on the acidity. Who's the food nerd now, you crusty old codger?

There have actually been major advances in our pursuit of coffee since we started traveling. Bean juice was always a means to an end, but, with the proliferation of Starbucks and the many independent shops around the country, this stimulating elixir is starting to actually taste pretty good. I don't have a refined enough palette to tell the good from the great, but I will definitely go out of my way to find the good over the shit. James still loves shit coffee. Even when we start carrying around our own pour-over rig, complete with conical grinder, he'll use the first Walmart stop to buy a twenty-dollar Mr. Coffee so he can drink his swill.

Cooking, the movement of it, becomes a meditation, a calming everyday practice that relieves my stress and worry. The moment I set foot onto that bus that meditation disappears. There is no stovetop on a tour bus, only a microwave inside of a highway-bound submarine. Here are the gastronomical smells that are appropriate on a tour bus: popcorn, beer, ramen, coffee, pizza, burrito, whiskey, soda, lemon or lime for cocktails, inoffensive cheese or deli meat, fruit, raw vegetables and eventually, kombucha. I attempt to cook raw shrimp in the microwave, which produces an odor so noxious that it drives my coworkers fleeing off into the night. I can't cook on tour, and it drives me nuts.

I do, however, take more note of restaurants. Don't ever ask the local crew "What's a good place to eat around here?" unless you're in a hurry. Their free time on any given night is extremely limited so they will only give recommendations that are within a two-minute walk and have quick turnaround service. This is mostly pizza, burritos and burgers, which are all delicious, but when you're an aspiring culinarian in a pre-Yelp world you've got to do more legwork.

Luckily, I am highly adept at walking aimlessly for hours in search of nothing. I need merely to wander until I find an establishment that both piques my interest and is very busy. Very busy either means very hip or, most likely, very good. Since I roll solo I can usually belly up to the bar, order a pint and ask the bartender what's good. They are often a fellow gastro adventurer and will certainly treat me right, especially if they know my band and I am happy to put them on the list for the show that night. This, not the hour onstage, is the moment that I feel most victorious.

I am also starting to experiment with destination dining when I am on the road. Not only do I have disposable income now, but I've also got time. The bus travels at night while we slumber. I wake late every morning in a new city. First thought, coffee. If the driver is worth his salt, he's prepped the drip with grounds and all is ready to perk. At the end of the first cup I must go on a mission. You can't shit on a tour bus since they have septic tanks that the driver has to clean, and any fecal matter is a five-hundred-dollar fine. Nobody tells you that a big part of bus touring is all the time spent trying to find a commode. Here's a tip: hotel lobbies have pretty decent toilets and, sometimes, free coffee. It's like trying to get backstage, just pretend you're supposed to be there and you'll be fine.

After this mission is accomplished it's time to find lunch. I've still got a few hours before load in and I'm all about the long walkabout, so let's go hunting. I start paying attention to the local fare. Crab in Baltimore, Bertha's Mussels, too. Cheesesteak in Philly. Hot Brown in Louisville. Chicago dogs,

Cincinnati chili, salmon in Seattle, sourdough bowl in San Francisco. My culinary awakening is in its infancy so it's pretty pedestrian.

I convince the driver to take us all to The Anchor Bar in Buffalo on a day off. The wings may not be the best, but this is where they were invented so I gotta make a pilgrimage at least once. The tour manager orders a dozen with the Anchor's signature suicidal sauce. "How much for you to down a shot glass of that shit, bud?" Between all of us at the table the pot grows to five hundo, but the waitress is reluctant. She's seen people attempt this kind of nonsense before.

After assuring her that we are very generous tippers, she concedes and brings the clear glass of liquid pain. The tour manager shoots it back and then a look befalls his face that telegraphs the immediate and obvious mistake. Within moments he is covered in sweat and sprints to the bathroom. We are howling with laughter. He spends the rest of the day sweating in his bunk, occasionally asking if we can pull into a truck stop for a few minutes.

James had been taking out an Ampeg 4×10 bass cabinet as a keyboard amp. We bought a pretty expensive road case for it, but now he's just going direct onstage and it's become obsolete. I repurpose the road case to fit my Weber kettle grill. If I take the legs off it's the perfect size to fit in the case. When I can, I take our buyout cash and buy groceries, grilling for all our crew and the house locals. The only problem is getting the thing to cool down enough to be able to load it back into the case. I take to leaving it out throughout the show and then disassembling the beast while still sweaty in my show clothes, but at least I get to cook something. It's a rare reprieve from the monotony of tour life. One that I welcome with open arms.

I've heard about the Pike Place Market stall where they throw the fish and freak out customers with the scary jaws of monkfish (the poor man's lobster) and I have to go there. We are playing Seattle and I make a pilgrimage to the market, down an oyster shot, and watch for a while. Wouldn't be a bad life, a fishmonger. I've thought this of butchers as well. There is just the task at hand. I'm a bit lost currently. My band is very successful, but I can't help but think that I've accomplished everything I set out to do, and now I'm at a loss for new challenges. Everything's kind of on autopilot right now and, I guess, I'm bored.

After watching the fishmongers, I decide to buy some product to send home via dry ice. Five hundred dollars and several guest list spots later, I've gotten a parcel of Alaskan king crab, coho salmon and the aforementioned monkfish sent back to my apartment. Side note: the fishmonger is the only positive monger. The other mongers are fear, hate and war, and those are no good for anyone.

During the show I can see the tattooed fish slinger as he crowd surfs towards the stage. It warms my heart. Our industries aren't that dissimilar and I'm glad I could give him a good time. Godspeed you, righteous fish man.

The Dunder Chee

I am pacing the floor of a lounge at Los Angeles International Airport having a panic attack on the phone with Our Manager. We are set to board a seventeen-hour flight to Sydney, Australia, and I desperately don't want to go. It's not that I don't want to go there, this is our first trip to Australia. It's not the band that we're opening for, they've been nothing but wonderful and are quite good. It's that I don't want to leave, at all. Something in me has changed. Some chemical in my brain has been released and I've literally come to despise the one thing I always wanted to do...tour.

Our Manager assures me that this tour will be a breeze. We've got our lunatic Australian tour manager whom we'll call The Aussie, Wonder Kid is doing sound, and the shows will all be huge. It's just so fucking far away. There seems to be a correlation between the distance I am from home and how unhappy I am. Europe is more difficult than the East Coast, and Australia is worse than Europe, at least in terms of my mental state. A few years later it will be Australia that ultimately breaks me, but for now I steady myself, hang up the phone, and get on the plane.

As we cross the International Date Line it's James' birthday, so we celebrate it twice. Eventually the flight staff cuts us off, but not before we get rip-roaring drunk enough to irritate everyone else on the plane. Then, a fitful, awkward sleep, sitting upright and waking suddenly every time my head drops to the side. This is murder on my neck but I can't ever get comfortable with those neck pillows. This is how I learned to sleep in the van, an hour at a time in the driver's seat at a rest stop. But this is many, many hours, so I sleep in many, many short shifts.

The Aussie—well, *our* Aussie, everyone here is an Aussie—is waiting for us at the terminal. We've travelled with him before, partied with him, attended his green card wedding to his drug dealer so he could stay in the States. We met him through Our Manager. He works for some friends' bands and seems to be the "work hard, play hard" type, but never until the job is done. This is a common trait in tour managers and can be the factor that separates the good from the bad. He can drink us under the table but never touches a drop until we've been paid and loaded out. I really like The Aussie but I think he's a fucking lunatic.

At baggage claim we are held up because there is a literal circus on this flight and all their custom-built acrobat bullshit is taking up the oversized baggage department. Depending on the airline or, let's be honest, the person working the baggage claim, sometimes our guitars and other instruments arrive on the carousel and sometimes in the oversize. We divide into two teams, each armed with roller carts, and wait with delegates at both locations. This time luggage is in one spot, gear is in the other, and this fucking circus is jamming up the flow. At customs and immigration they seem real hopped up on not bringing in wildlife or plants, that's a new twist. They have more beasts that can kill you here than anywhere in the world, why do they care what we bring in?

Once we finally get outside and everyone has a chance to smoke we push our carts to the sprinter van that will be our chariot for the next month. Most Australian tours are fly-ins. American bands typically only play the five major cities, but they are too far apart from one another to drive. Each show day would be followed by three days off on the road, and that's more expensive than just flying to every gig. But we're opening for an Australian band and they are playing every backwater in this country. Every other time we come here we'll stay for four or five days, but this time we're here for a month and we're not even doing the full tour.

Support gigs, like festivals, are incredibly easy and honestly pretty boring. You only really need to be at work for an hour and there's just too much time to kill. Idle hands are the devil's playthings, after all. The first day, The Aussie takes us to the beach and we go swimming in the ocean. It's not until we walk back to the van that we see the "Danger: Shark-Infested Waters" sign and shudder to think what carnage we just avoided.

We tend to roll up an hour before doors, push onto the stage, line check and then clock in. "Clocking in" means cracking your first beer, which on this trip seems to be a noxious brew called Victoria Bitter. They don't actually like Fosters here, we're told, that's just an American marketing campaign. The locals just call the green bottles "Vee Bee," and one colorful promoter tells us it stands for "Vaginal Backwash." How quaint.

The problem with clocking in before a support slot is that you've still got so much of the night left to ruin. Since I only have to sing for thirty minutes every night on this run I can actually hang out after the show without losing my voice. But my attitude quickly turns sour if I've had a few and I get homesick. We've got three happy drunks, one mean drunk, and me...the sad drunk.

Sad drunks are a bad hang and my mood is not enhanced by these shows. These are large, sometimes over a thousand people, sold out, but we're the first of three bands and unknown except to a minority of hipsters who get what's going on in the States. This room holds fifteen hundred people and they are all at the bar, save ten or fifteen diehards at the front of the stage. We've taken to opening the set with the ballad we usually close with, because who the fuck cares? Nobody is listening to us. In a mere three years from now we'll be headlining these same sold-out venues, but on this trip it's crickets. Maybe I was right to want to stay home.

I think the easiest way to sum up Australians is by discussing their sports. They equally love cricket, that most proper of dances, and Aussie rules football, which makes pro wrestling look like ballet. Australia is both breathtakingly beautiful and spectacularly violent, from the aforementioned zoological predators to the human inhabitants themselves. Head butts are not uncommon in bar fights and are even given lovingly sometimes. I've been called a "cunt" and a "dickhead" by friends and fans alike. Those would be fighting words back home, but here they are terms of affection.

They don't have The Bell here, or really any Mexican food at all. We couldn't be further from the source, but that never stopped us from having burritos in Germany. We finally find the only outlet in Sydney. Pilgrims, we descend upon the shrine and eat our fill. When we travel internationally we eat like locals 99% of the time, but sometimes you just want a bean burrito in Oz or a Whopper in Tokyo. There's nothing wrong with the occasional taste of home. This might be the best seven-layer I've ever had in my life and now I'm gonna give myself a hernia trying to sing with this torpedo in my stomach.

Because of some sort of artist's discount granted by the Australian government, or maybe it was some scam that The Aussie was pulling, we're staying in really nice hotels. Four-star affairs, with pools, near the ocean. I have no idea why anyone would want to swim in a man-made pool when they could dance in the waves. The downside to staying in these nicer digs is paying for the amenities. The business traveller Holiday Inns we're accustomed to have both free parking and breakfast, even if that breakfast is modest. In these swanky high-thread-count joints we have to pay for both.

Shit's expensive down here. All I want is a Caesar salad and it's twenty-five clams, it doesn't even have chicken on it or anything. This becomes our new metric regarding the cost of things. As in, "How'd we do in merch last night?" "Not great, about eight Caesar salads." This means about two hundo, which on this tour isn't that bad, but back home it's peanuts. Peanuts, you say? Well that would put you back a quarter Caesar salad.

Here's what I've learned so far on this beautiful island. If you order a burger with everything on it this includes a giant slice of red beet. Everything possible is shortened using the suffix "ie." So breakfast is "brekkie," etc. They do say "g'day" and call everyone "mate," but no mention of "barbies" or shrimp. Any nickname will include the letter "o" at the end: Rob-o, Jim-o, Nick-o. Instead of "don't worry about it," they are fond of saying "no worries," or the more emphatic "no fucking worries, mate." I'm sure we're not the first to think of it, but we've taken to saying "no wucking furries" instead. An abundance of anything is translated to "heaps," as in "there's heaps of shops on that street over there."

There is a special work visa that makes it easier for Canadian and British bands to tour here, and vice versa. Therefore the occasional Canadian group that might be worth nothing in the States could be really huge in Oz. We learn from a map in a pub on Sydney Harbor that the entire continent of Europe would fit inside this country, it being a continent itself. There is a small portion of the country in the north that operates within a time zone thirty minutes later than its nearest neighbor. I don't know of anywhere else on earth where they do that. What a pain that must be if you have to go there very often, to remember that everything is a half hour off.

The city of Perth, where the headliner of this tour are from, is the only major metropolis on the west side of the country, and it's the only part of the tour we're not doing. We're not driving all the way across the outback for one gig. Said band's manager has a third nipple and used to work on a farm where his job was to fire a shotgun to scare off kangaroos, which are apparently mean fuckers. Koalas are as well.

The main support on this tour is an Aussie ska outfit. The lead singer has a pompadour and must come from money. He shelled out the enormous expense to not only purchase a 1960s Cadillac and have it shipped here, he also had it customized to put the steering wheel on the other side to comply with Australian vehicle standards. We've never toured with a ska band before, barely ever played with any. Nothing against the genre, it just hasn't happened often. I keep thinking, "Why would you want to have so many mouths to feed?" You'd burn straight through your guarantee just to pay the band, let alone the crew. It was a hard enough sell to add James full time, therefore reducing each of our cut by 5%, but that's still better than an eight-piece band or more. Just can't justify the math in my head.

When one travels, it is customary to listen the local music of whatever territory you're visiting. Whether it's Nirvana in Seattle or The 'Mats in Minneapolis, it's just an appropriate way to put yourself in the mood of the city, or in this case, the continent. The Aussie has been trying to get us to listen to some old school Australian punk and metal bands that we've never heard of and honestly have no interest in. We want to listen to Bon Scott. I admit to the group that when I was a kid I never knew what he was saying in "Dirty Deeds Done Dirt Cheap" until I saw the album artwork. I thought he was saying some gibberish word like "dunder chee" instead of the much more obvious "done dirt cheap." Thus, the legend of the Dunder Chee, a mythical creature that haunted New South Wales and brought good children gifts in the night, was born. I think I'm starting to go a little mad on this tour.

One show, on the Gold Coast, has a barricade that runs at a forty-five-degree angle down the middle of the crowd, separating the drunks from the kids. Therefore, the handful of people who are watching us are all in front of me while no one is in front of Jim. This whole trip is very humbling after the last couple of runs in Europe and the States.

In the States our second record seems to have legs in an indie rock sense. Our headlining shows are growing in size, not quickly enough to feel strange, there's just more people each time we come through town. Since we come through most major cities at least two or three times a year it's starting to add up. (People keep telling us they heard us on a skate video or a BMX video or something like that. I don't know anything about that particular brand of marketing, but apparently we owe those videos a great debt for our success.)

That's what makes this tour particularly disheartening. We've been touring for almost three years straight and I am burned out. The lack of interest from the crowd makes the whole thing more difficult. Still, I do what I always do and sing my guts out to the ten people who are there to see us. They'll get to brag to their friends in a couple of years about how they saw us play to like, nobody, but it was awesome.

The tour is making a stop at a festival in Adelaide, which is in the province of South Australia, named such even though the province of Victoria is even further south. Non-locals apparently call it "Murder-laide" because it has the highest death count in the country. Stranger still, the festival is in an old jail, or "gaol" as it was written when this country was founded. This site is a historic monument and all the dressing rooms are in the old cells. We are instructed not to deface any of the racist graffiti as this is a museum and they want to keep it intact. There's some pretty burly shit on these walls and it's hard to resist the temptation to correct it, but we manage to not edit the text.

A local animal handler has brought a sedated koala to the communal backstage area and people are lined up to hold it. This seem particularly grotesque to me. I'm not really even a fan of zoos, I'm not going to play with a wild animal that has been drugged for my entertainment. It's about a hundred and ten degrees when we play outside at midday but at least there are people to watch us. Not fans necessarily, just festival goers, but they are enthusiastic. After our set we bid farewell to our hosts and make our way to the airport to do the whole dance again but in reverse.

On the flight home I actually sleep. Not fitfully, not drunkenly. It is the sleep of the dead. It's been a month since I've even had the time for a full forty winks, and this plane may as well be the Four Seasons.

When we're back at home, I hang out with Wonder Kid and he shows me some new music. He doesn't really have much of a punk background. His older brother plays a mean train beat in an alt-country outfit. I guess this is technically "cow punk," but that term always sounded like a novelty to me.

We listen to a lot of singer/songwriters, which is a genre unto itself as well as a job description. I'm a singer and a songwriter, but I'm not a singer/songwriter. Why is that? Nowadays they call it "Americana." That's a little better, I guess. Its roots are in American folk music, which has its roots in Irish and English ballads, so maybe "Post-Colonial" should be in there somewhere. I'm drawn to this music in the same way I originally was to punk rock. It's very honest and simple and pure. It's also very driven by lyrics, which I've been focusing more and more on.

I've always written lyrics that are fairly obtuse. I think of them as cryptic, but people often figure them out, or figure something out, even if it's inaccurate. The lyrics in these singer/songwriters' songs are poetic, but it's not as difficult to ascertain their meaning. I've been writing in a kind of code, but these songs are nothing like that. I'm struck by how powerful they can be by being quiet. These songs can make you cry without the singer ever raising their voice. I've always treated volume as a way to achieve dynamics, the quiet parts being there to make the loud parts more bombastic.

Honestly, I'm ready for this right now. The few years we've been touring have been exhausting, and a lot of the bands we play with sound very similar. Some say they sound similar to us, but since I can hear all our influences in the songs we write I don't see it that way. It would be more accurate to say they sound similar to the bands we're ripping off.

187   In the coming years the industry will take notice and a lot of the bands we play with now will start to be exploited. Some to greater success than others. I truly have no interest in that. We tried going down that corporate road once before and it left a bad taste in my mouth. The coming new wave of money, and therefore influence from those lending the money, will push me deeper and deeper into this quieter genre. Plus, it's the anti-ska business model. You can literally do it by yourself.

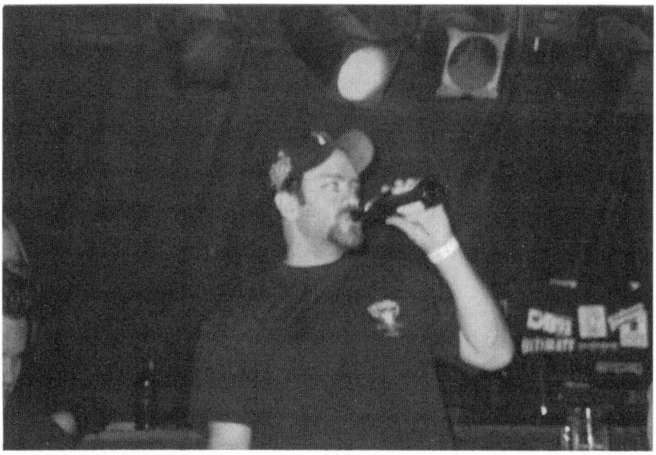

Shabu Shabu

In an airplane over the sea. I am thirty-seven thousand feet above the Pacific Ocean, three thousand miles from American soil. It's our first trip to Japan and the sixteen-hour flight is wearing on me greatly. Sake helps, hot towels are nice. We're supposed to be sleeping, the cabin lights have been dimmed, and most people have their windows closed. I keep mine open and stare out into the darkness, unable to rest.

I imagine that I can see the ocean. The flight map says we're about halfway there. This is before the advent of individual free entertainment in the headrest of the seat in front of you. There is one large screen at the front of the cabin that alternates between a map of our progress and a report of our altitude and the distance from our point of departure to our destination. Eventually this screen will attempt to entertain us with a bad Jackie Chan film, but until then I am stuck with my Vonnegut book.

I'm fully aware of this milestone. We are the first band that we know, the first of our peers, to make this journey to Asia. I literally have no idea what to expect. The only stories I've heard of tours over here were from hair metal bands I read about in *RIP Magazine*. Something about the six-foot-tall bleached blonde guitarist from Ratt sticking out in a crowd. Somehow I don't think the sexual exploits of that lifestyle will translate, but maybe the intoxicant intake will be comparable. I've been told they are hardcore about marijuana in this country, it's not to be fucked with. That shouldn't be a problem for me.

The five of us have brought The Aussie, Wonder Kid and Mr. Happy. There is no professional reason for Mr. Happy to be here, and, though I doubt he would admit it, he's excited by this milestone, too. We're certainly the first of his bands to do this, we're his first band to do a lot of things. We are the rock upon which he will build his church. I'm glad that he's here, having a native New Yorker in your crew is probably a good asset your first time in Tokyo. Navigating a city that size is not for the faint of heart.

James is dead out. He, Jim and I all hate flying. James self-medicates with a heroic dose of this, that or the other to knock his ass out for the duration of the trip. He's got the aisle seat, and the stranger next to him has to climb over his comatose corpse to get to the toilet. Jim and I are just drinking, the hope being that the alcohol combined with altitude will eventually lull us to sleep. But, so far, no luck.

We land at Narita International Airport dazed and confused. Immigration and customs are quick and efficient like most things here. We are greeted by the promoter rep named Nori and our label rep named Emiko. We're actually on a major label in Japan, the only time that's ever happened. We can officially call ourselves a real band since we're technically on a major. Jokingly we refer to our two very successful independent albums as "demos." This is the big time. Though we are licensed to several other indie labels in other territories around the world, here we're big shit, I guess.

We gather all our luggage, guitars, keyboards and drums. With several carts full of instruments we stop at one of the many airport bodegas to pick up a couple six packs of Sapporo. Thank God, we've got an hour-plus drive to the hotel and we're all wide fucking awake. This plan will backfire spectacularly when we are stuck in Shibuya traffic with bladders full of beer and nowhere to unleash it. It is an abdominal hell.

The cab van that we are loaded into is clean and cramped. We are on top of each other for the ride. I ask the guys about a mutual friend's upcoming wedding and realize that it's on December seventh. I immediately note to the group that the date is both my grandfather's birthday and Pearl Harbor Day, forgetting just what country we are currently visiting. Everyone gives me a glare of absolute death and, realizing my mistake, I glance to the cab driver. Either he didn't hear me or doesn't speak English, most likely he's incredibly polite and professional, but still I feel like an ass. I'm sure we're not the first ugly Americans he's had in his cab.

Between the influence of The Photographer and Anthony Bourdain, I've always tried to be a traveler and not a tourist. That doesn't mean I won't see the sights, but I never want to be the ugly American. If anything, I will play the ignorant fool who can't speak the language and hope for the pity of whomever I must interact with. I know how to say "thank you" in many languages, it being the one thing I say from the stage besides the name of the band. In the coming years, as our country's predilection for war and arrogance becomes more prevalent, I'll come to tell shopkeepers that I'm Canadian. Everyone loves a Canadian, and most people can't tell an American apart from a Canadian unless they're wearing a football jersey, which I would never do.

I know that sometimes I can come across as the ugly American. It's usually under stressful travel situations and almost always due to a lack of sleep. Because I have to demand a schedule for meals, both because of my disease and because of performing, I sometimes come across like a diva. Our translator tells the guys I'm the second most difficult person she's ever worked with. She won't say who the number one is. I must have been in a particular mood that day, for that I am truly sorry.

Sleep, especially on international tours, is an unaffordable luxury. I guess if you never wanted to experience the city or attempt to have a good time you could get your eight hours in, but what a boring life that would be. I've been to a lot of places all over the world, but I've truly seen very few. I can tell you all about the van, the club, the restaurant and the hotel in several major metropolises, but only the places where I've stayed behind after a tour can I say I've truly experienced.

Eating, at least for me, is a similar conundrum. I'm still using the insulin that takes thirty minutes to activate, so the timing of meals is tricky. I try to keep a three-hour window between dinner and show time. Regardless of what I eat, this seems to be enough time for my food to digest before I have to scream for ninety minutes. Anything less than that amount of time and I will have to restrict my intake, sticking mainly to protein. Our gigs are a workout, especially for me and Ryan. The whole band is often drenched in sweat by the end of a set, but it's guaranteed that he and I will be soaked even if we're playing outside in the cold.

In Shibuya, the night club district of Tokyo, there are already people waiting for us at the hotel. Fans, all femme, giggle modestly and give us presents. How do they know where our hotel is? No matter, they are very nice, and I get some toe socks and other tchotchkes, so I'm happy to take pictures and sign whatever they want me to sign.

We are each given our own incredibly tiny room. I've never had my own room on tour before. When we graduated to even affording hotel rooms we would double up, or even triple up. The rooms are nice if simple. Buckwheat pillows (Mr. Happy loves these things for some reason), rabbit ear televisions, green tea and a fridge full of Asahi. All the creature comforts covered. It's midday but I try to get some sleep. As exhausted as I am, I can't drift off, so I wander the streets of Shibuya.

Shibuya is everything you would think it would be: neon signs, techno blaring, a thousand people crossing the intersection in one horde. Today the sky is grey as the looming clouds drop a steady trickle of rain down on the populace. The wall of umbrellas is reminiscent of the Spartans' interlocking shield defense formation. I don't mind a little rain but I do pull up the hood of my jacket. As I keep pace with the crowd

I am repeatedly poked in the face and eyes by the head-level umbrellas of the diminutive general public. I've never been tall before, I think to myself.

Lobby call at 6:00 p.m. to meet with Nori and his stage manager, Now. I realize at this moment that I'm unsure how to spell his name in print, but it's pronounced "NOW." He has a long goatee and a shaved head, like a Japanese Layne Staley. Technical logistics are discussed. This is really for our tour manager and sound guy, but we're all awake anyway so might as well attend the meeting. Nori and Now depart, and we're left on our own to fend for our supper.

Six Kansans, one native New Yorker and an Aussie descend on Shibuya in an attempt to find sustenance. I don't know how we decide on this particular restaurant, but we descend below street level into a fairly elaborately adorned establishment. There are no other patrons, which is never a good sign, but we are famished so we grab a table. We don't speak any Japanese and they don't speak any English, but somehow it is communicated that we want to order dinner.

A placeholder in the table is removed to reveal a burner, a pot of water is placed on it, and the burner is set alight. Not sure what this is, my only experience with tableside Japanese dining is with Hibachi grills, not soup. The staff brings us out several plates of cut vegetables and very thinly sliced, very marbled beef, along with several dipping sauces on the side. We are shown how to briefly wave the food through the boiling water, cooking it quickly, and then dip it in the sauce.

It's communal eating, not something we ever do back home, and it is simple, clean and perfect. We collectively grab our chopsticks and dig into the bounty, it is glorious. Shabu shabu, they call it. We drink endless beers and call for more meat like a Victorian king. We are all slaphappy with jet lag and excitement. What a lovely accident. How did we end up in this restaurant on the other side of the world together, sharing a communal meal delivered in a language we can't understand? Be a traveler, not a tourist. You just let the city take the lead on the dance floor. Sometimes it's magical, sometimes it's not, but in this particular moment all is right with the world.

After dinner we stumble back to the hotel and stop at a convenience store for snacks and more libations. As anyone who's been to Japan can tell you, the convenience stores are next level. You can actually get really good food at these neon bodegas. It's here that we learn about what might be the most brilliant invention since the wheel…the hot can.

In the Land of the Rising Sun they take coffee very seriously. They are a nation fueled by stimulants, primarily cigarettes and bean juice. The bodegas all have small hot boxes, like mini fridges but to keep things hot. Inside these warming stations they store good coffee in aluminum cans, keeping the coffee piping hot without ever burning it like percolators in the States. This is literally "good" gas station coffee and the very concept breaks my brain. Since I'm the only one who doesn't smoke, inevitably someone will pop in for darts and I'll pipe up, "Grab me a can." By the time they return the scalding liquid will have cooled to a manageable temperature. Hot can fresh out of the box will burn your taste buds off, that's a fact.

After our successful round of commerce at the bodega, The Aussie has a strange look in his eye. He walks up to two random women and puts his arm around them. I am mortified by this behavior but I soon learn that these are ladies of the night and they welcome his advances. "She's got a tongue ring, mate," he proudly brags to me. "Great," I reply, not knowing why that's important information. Back at the hotel he knocks on my door and thrusts his computer bag into my chest. "They may get me money, but they ain't gettin' me laptop" is the only thing he says, and he's off into the wind. He's a wild one, The Aussie. He can be a lot, but he's got a heart of gold.

The next morning we are met in the lobby by Nori and Emiko and we head to the train station. We board the bullet train to

Osaka with our luggage. Our instruments and merch are being van driven by Now but we travel in style. The sprawling city fades to countryside as the fog rolls over the hills. We sit back and try to rest, maybe get a bento box and a beer, not a bad way to tour if you get the chance.

Taking insulin on a train, even one as smooth as this one, can be challenging. I'm always scared of hitting a rough patch of track and hurting myself during the injection. I've had some bad experiences with injections during turbulence on planes. It feels more stable if I sit down to do it and get it over with as quickly as possible.

We arrive at the Osaka station and take two cabs to Club Quattro, the venue where we are performing tonight. It gets kind of confusing because all three clubs we are playing on this trip (Osaka, Nagoya, and two nights in Tokyo) are Club Quattro locations. The only time we've played the same venue in different cities in the States is House of Blues, but this is way different. For starters, there is about a stadium's amount of lights on this stage. The entire wall behind us is covered in park hands. It's as if it was our backdrop, somehow spelling out the band's name. I shudder to think how brutally hot the stage is going to be, but what's that? They are LED lights? They don't give off any heat? Hell yeah, I love this place.

We set our bags backstage and are greeted with a spread of sushi and beer. Can we only tour in Japan, please? Onstage we set up the rental gear, it's not exactly the same stuff we've got back home but it will do the trick. We sound check with Wonder Kid on the faders, and then the strangest thing happens. All the stagehands—and there are a lot—start taking Polaroid pictures of our amps, where the dials are set, where our pedal boards are placed and which way the knobs on any given pedal are facing. They take pictures of the drums, how they are set up, the keyboards, where all the mics are placed, and how tall the vocal mic stands are. They even go out to the sound board and take photos of how the mix is set. Over the coming days we will arrive at each show to find all our gear set up and dialed in, as well as the sound board. This is attention to detail I've never even thought of, let alone seen before.

The show starts, the crowd is amazing. They sing every song, and come to collectively shout "hey hey hey" on every downbeat without vocals. When a song ends they applaud uproariously for five seconds and then become completely silent. This catches us off guard, it's like a library in here. What's going on? They are so quiet I think they can hear us talking onstage, start the next fucking song quick. We play the bonus track from the Japanese-only version of the album and the place goes absolutely batshit. We walk offstage victorious and drenched. What the hell just happened?

After the show, dinner is a communal affair. The eight of us, plus Nori, Now, Emiko and our translator, as well as some of the local crew, all discard our shoes and sit down on pillows around a single table. Emiko and Nori order for all of us. Takoyaki, an Osaka specialty, octopus balls. Pieces of the cephalopod dipped in batter and fried in a special pan. Yakitori grilled over charcoal, something called "soft bone" which seems to be fried cartilage. Of course, I'm the one who wants to try all the weird stuff. Uni (sea urchin), Unagi (eel), chicken feet, bring it on. I ask Emiko if she can take me to get Fugu, the poisonous blowfish native to Japan that I've learned about from cooking shows. She laughs at me, I guess it would be a bad look for her if the lead singer of the band she was shepherding ended up in the hospital, or worse, because of her willingness to indulge his desire for dangerous culinary adventures.

There is drinking, a lot of drinking. The Japanese do not fuck around when it comes to alcohol. The trains stop running at midnight and start up again at 5:00 a.m., so if you wanna get home you either gotta call it early or double down 'til the sun comes up. These fools are doubling down. Nori sways as he speaks to Now at a rapid pace. Suddenly Nori pulls out a pocket knife, grabs Now by the beard and cuts it off, laughing like a madman the whole time. We are stunned, not sure what is going to happen, but Now busts out laughing. I guess if your drunk boss cuts off your beard, really, what can you do? One of the guys from the opening bands sets his pubic hair on fire at the table. This is also, apparently, an Osaka thing.

Afterwards it's back to the hotel to slumber on an uncomfortable buckwheat pillow. I awake in the middle of the night unable to sleep. They say it takes one day for every time zone you've travelled through to completely get over jet lag, so I should be acclimated in a little over two weeks, but we're only in Japan for six days. I get dressed and head out into the night still buzzed from dinner.

It is many, many hours until I can call home, and I feel very, very alone. Even in this wash of humanity I am an island in the sea and I'm scared of my own thoughts. I'm scared because I don't know what to do with myself, both in this moment and with my life moving forward. Sleep deprivation can play wicked tricks on your mind, and I'm sure my exhausted state is only exacerbating the situation.

For the last decade, since I was twelve years old, this has been all I've ever wanted to do. I came at this work with a laser focus and would stop at nothing until the job was finished. But how do you know when the job is finished? I've heard people say workaholics are the only addicts that are celebrated at the height of their addiction. Maybe I need to go cold turkey?

People have been singing along with me at shows for a while. They didn't do that in the beginning, nobody knew our songs. Something's changed, though. I'm seeing tattoos of our album art, or even stranger, my lyrics, on more and more bodies. I like tattoos and don't really buy into the logic that it's something you'll regret when you're older. I figure it's a document of a time and place in life, so if that's how you wanna mark the occasion you should do it. Having said that, it's a strange concept to wrap my head around that anyone would want to permanently scar themselves with something that I wrote about my life.

Those songs are for me, they don't have anything to do with you, I think to myself. This is, of course, a naive way of thinking. Once you release a record into the world you cease having ownership of it. It becomes the property of the listener, and they are free to interpret it any way they choose. They are also free to celebrate it any way they want, and if that means getting my self-reflective gibberish inked across their neck then that's their prerogative.

I'm starting to become more of a showman, at least I'm starting to be more conscious of it. The crowds are big enough now that stage banter isn't really a conversation, it's more me making declarative statements and asking hack questions like, "You having a good time tonight?" This aspect of the job is starting to lose its luster. I have a friend in another band who has a combative relationship with their audience. Not that they are mean to them, just that they see the crowd as something to be conquered, and prepare themselves for battle accordingly. I don't want to be that kind of performer, that's not why I got into this in the first place. Besides loving music (that should go without saying) I got into this because of the community. It was the place where I finally fit in, where we were all equals. The band and the crowd at a basement show are literally on the same level, and it's the floor. I'm now elevated to some sort of musical business class and I'm feeling more and more out of touch with the people in coach.

I want to be crystal clear here, I don't dislike the audience. If anything I feel a responsibility to them, especially as ticket prices are starting to rise. I want them to forget their problems for ninety minutes and have a good time. I want to be their escape. But it's not a community anymore, it's us and them. We've surpassed most of our contemporaries as far as album and ticket sales go, and I'm starting to feel those resentments. Perfectly normal feelings, I understand, but it's changed the nature of our relationships. Bands we've done house-show tours with are now opening for us. We've gone from being equals to being members of different castes.

All of this is heightening my anxiety. I feel ashamed of our success around friends, and defensive about it to the press and public. I do feel distant from the audience, sometimes literally. We're always on a stage, often one that's too tall and protected by a barricade. It's hard to feel close to people when you're surrounded by security.

These thoughts are still running through my brain later as I wander the streets of Tokyo after the train ride from Osaka. I've gotten lost several times, which is usually fun but can be kind of terrifying here. As long as I can find the Hachiko statue I know I am safe. The faithful dog who waited for his master at the Shibuya train station even after his death. I relate to this dog, doing the same thing over and over every day though it ceases to accomplish anything. His master, just like the person I was and the scene that I came from, are never coming back.

The writing is on the wall. Those same major labels that disregarded us—or worse, treated us like kids—are starting to work with our younger contemporaries. Soon there will be label bidding wars and expensive music videos made for this supposedly new style of music. This tour is the end (or so we think) of a whirlwind that has taken us all over the world. Our gamble on Our Manager's tiny little label has paid off, our bet on ourselves is paying big dividends. We aren't going anywhere, nobody is going to offer us a better deal than we already have. But there's blood in the water and the sharks are circling. It's only a matter of time before this whole thing breaks big.

When I can finally call Honey White I explain my existential thoughts. She's in a similar situation. She's about to graduate and, though she wants to continue on to get her PhD, she's kind of hitting a similar burnout point. She's always been laser focused on academia. I think it's one of the things that drew us to each other, me with music and her with school. How many teenagers do you know who already have a clear vision of what they intend to do with the rest of their life? We decide to take some time off at home to plan the wedding and figure out our next move.

On the last day in Tokyo, Mr. Happy, Wonder Kid and I take the train to the Imperial Palace. Somehow we navigate the station even though nothing is written in English, we just have to memorize the shapes of the kanji. Walking around those majestic grounds, I confide in them that this trip was the last thing on my list. Japan was the last frontier that I fantasized about touring when I was a kid. I'm not sure what to do now. Mr. Happy shrugs and suggests, "I guess you just do it all again."

I know he's right, but a feeling of defeat washes over me. This is the end of the adventure and the beginning of this being a job. It is in this moment that I know my life is gonna change, but I'm not sure how. I really hadn't thought past this point. I think about this on the flight home, over and over again. Where do we go from here?

Every Double Life

I am sitting in the bedroom of the apartment in Allston, Rock City, that I share with Honey White and Our Mutual Best Friend. Kitty the house cat stares at me contemplatively while I repeatedly pound out a melody on my Fender Rhodes electric piano. I don't play piano, but I don't play guitar very well either. Both are just tools, a means to an end to find a song.

Songwriting, at least for me, is about seventy-five percent repetition and twenty-five percent inspiration. I think of it as a muscle that I'm trying to maintain, if I stop for too long it will atrophy. I know it sounds crazy but I've found that I always get new inspiration from different instruments. Even picking up a different guitar can spark something. It's as if the song was in the instrument all along, even though that sounds like hippie nonsense.

I've found that writing on the Rhodes has produced a similar kind of creative spark. James has been playing one on the road, and I'll sit and tinker with it before sound check. The touring rig is complete with original speaker cabinet, but I ended up buying a less elaborate model for my bedroom. The instrument on the left-hand side has a moody, dark sound, and I've been writing things that are less loud, fast and angry, and more quiet and introspective. Wonder Kid's record collection has quickly become similar to my own, and I'm toying with the idea of recording a record by myself.

The band writes collaboratively, Jim or I will bring either a complete song or just a melody or riff to the group and we'll bang it out. It isn't finished until we've all put our own stink on it, so it's best not to be too precious with your compositions when presenting them to the guys. Songs will get chopped and twisted and may lose all of my original intention, but that's alright. That's just the way we do it, and it works.

It is, however, an intimidating proposition to present a song that I am really in love with which might be dismissed out of hand before we even start working on it. It's also a very taxing way to work, as I'm constantly having to defend the parts of the songs that I desperately don't want to change. Besides wanting to try a different style of song, I want to make something that I have complete control over.

I did this once before when Secular Theme disbanded. When that unit dissolved I felt like I was helpless, like there was no way I could play music without Rambo being the whirlwind center of attention. After a moment of self-pity I decided that I at least had to try to do it on my own, I had to prove to myself that he wasn't the only reason I could play music. So I started putting together a new band, and then another, and then another, until finally getting it right. Now I wanted to prove to myself that I could do it alone, without the band. I wasn't unhappy with the group but I was up for the challenge.

At the Hurricane, I had ceremoniously declared, "If I ever start a side project it's gonna be called The New Amsterdams." I had been obsessed with Elvis Costello for a while at that point, and with that song in particular. It is customary in our scene that if someone is going to perform by themselves they don't do it under their own name. It's one of those punk rock rules that nobody really gives a shit about anymore. So even though this was going to be a solo venture it had to have a band name. The title being plural, even though the band was just one person, didn't even occur to me at the time.

After my long days walking around the city, and before I would start cooking dinner, I would sit down at the Rhodes and attempt to write something. I would then transpose the song to guitar so that I could actually play it and sing it at the same time, and record it on an analog Tascam four-track recorder. I would do one track of the song live as I sang it, a second track for a harmony vocal, a third track for the piano, and the final track for a lead line on either guitar or the Rhodes. When I've got about twenty songs finished in this style, I call Wonder Kid and tell him to book a studio for us to record an album. It will be just us, me performing and him engineering in a small studio in Lawrence, directly above a diner.

At the end of a raucous European tour in the spring, Honey White and I stay on the continent for two more weeks to see her family's native country and visit a friend in Paris. She's just graduated so the timing is perfect. She flies to Germany to meet us, and after the last two festivals we hop on a train to Poland. Our sleeper car is barely held together with duct tape but it doesn't matter. When we cross over the border in the middle of the night (Poland wasn't in the EU yet) we are awoken by guards who laugh at an American with a Polish last name. That's why we're here, dickhead.

We explore Warsaw and Krakow, eat pierogies, drink beer and copulate like rabbits in heat. We visit Częstochowa, where the painting of the Black Madonna lives, a portrait supposedly painted by Saint Luke the Evangelist. There are many Americans lingering at the Pauline monastery of Jasna Góra. We are asked if we are Catholic pilgrims or missionaries like them. Why else would an American be in this town only known for a religious relic? We're just stopping here to check out this painting on our way to Oświęcim. We're gonna go to see Auschwitz. On that particular train ride, I can't help but feel disturbed that these are the same tracks that were used in the war. The museum is nestled in the middle of the town, you can see kids playing football in the lot across the street. The normalcy of the whole place is haunting.

After a brief stop in Prague, and more marathon lovemaking, Honey White isn't feeling so well. Turns out she's got a urinary tract infection, probably from our incessant lascivious activities. She is ill the whole train to Paris, where we are staying with a friend of hers from university that is living as an ex-pat in the city. A doctor is called and he smokes a cigarette as he examines her. He prescribes antibiotics, and within a day or so she's up on her feet again exploring the city with me.

After Paris we fly back to Boston and load up a box truck with Our Mutual Best Friend and a terrified cat to make the fourteen-hundred-mile drive home. After a brief stay at her parents we move to Lawrence to plan the wedding. The plan is to only stay here long enough to save up money to move to New York, but we'll see. I'm hoping she falls in love with the place like I have. We move into the bottom half of a duplex on Kentucky Street right in the heart of the student ghetto. I set up the Rhodes and the four-track and try to whittle down the list of songs to ten. It ultimately becomes a twelve track album with a studio-written power pop number, which originally goes unlisted, and an Afghan Whigs cover that is one of Honey White's favorite songs.

In the studio I eventually agree to let some of the songs have a full band arrangement. This wasn't my original intent but I concede, maybe the record will be boring if it's just me and a guitar. Rob is brought in to play bass. Our friend Jake (who makes the drums with his dad) will keep the beat and Wonder Kid will be on keys, he's actually a good pianist. Ed Rose, who produced our early EPs, comes in to lay down a wicked guitar solo, and James attempts to play the cello. We ultimately end up using samples for any strings.

Earlier in the year on a particularly raucous night off in New York, we'd been enjoying libations with Mr. Happy at our favorite haunt in his neighborhood. It was a quiet bar, at least during the week, and I was drinking whiskey and playing pool. The drummer of a band I'm still infatuated with, one that had a profound influence on me, was nursing an Old Overholt at the bar. I offered to buy his drink and proceeded to drunkenly tell him how important his band is, that we wouldn't be where we are without them.

"Yeah, I bet you wouldn't," he retorted in a surly tone that I didn't take offense to. He had an air of bitterness, and meeting a younger, more successful musician rubbed him the wrong way even though I was buying the drinks. I was giddy and too plastered to even notice that he was repeatedly insulting me. Finally Mr. Happy, who was more cognizant of this transgression than I, dragged me out of the bar and off to bed. The next morning over eggs and hangovers he walked through the night with me. I was heartbroken and vowed to never treat a fan like that. I wrote "Never Treat Others" that night.

I won't go through every song on the record, but two are notable to this story. "Every Double Life" is a meditation on how different my life had become when I wasn't on the road. I had become fairly domestic, obsessively cooking and getting ready to be married. It's hard for me to live as two things simultaneously, at least in my head. It's even more disorienting given that I now have an onstage personality as well. It's a kind of code switching between the band-me and the me-me, if that makes any sense. The fact that it seems to mimic a song by the Arizona band is an accident.

"Proceed With Caution" is foreboding. Everything was going really well both personally and professionally. I'm not the self-sabotaging type but I can't help feeling like the other shoe is gonna drop soon. We can't continue to accidentally do everything correctly forever, right? In the coming years both my career and my family will be shaken up, and the marriage of the two will become infinitely more complicated, but that's a story for another time.

The record, *Never You Mind*, was finished that summer and released in September. No tour was planned around the release because of my pending nuptials. The record didn't exactly come out the way I had envisioned, the same way the band's first album hadn't. But it is a valiant effort, and I was, in the end, able to prove to myself that I could do it. After it was finished I immediately started writing its successor, which I was adamant would be a solo-only affair as a point of principle. I still had more stories to tell.

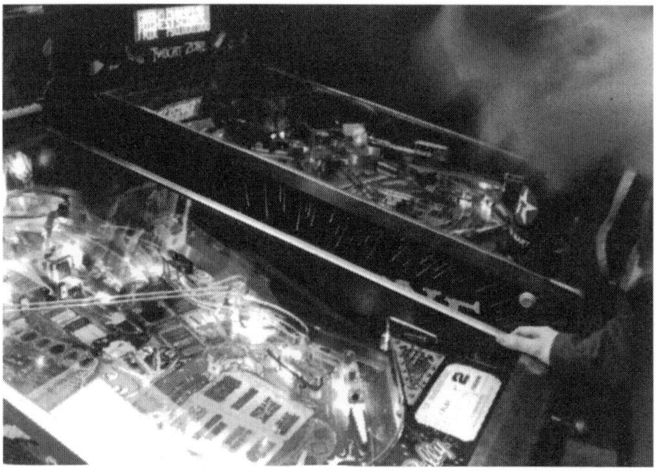

Red Letter Days

New Year's Eve after a brief stint at the bar, Honey White and I end up at a house party. Later that night we both try cocaine for the first time with some more experienced friends. I immediately realize that this is the best drug ever invented and that I will never, can never, do it again. I write seven songs that night and demo them all on the Tascam. In the light of day the next afternoon I delete them all, the wretched compositions a reminder of my decision that this drug was something I could really, really get into, and it wouldn't end well. That pretty much set the tone for the coming year.

The hockey bus pulls up in front of The Bottleneck well before it is time to load in. This is no ordinary tour vehicle, this was designed for a sports team. Besides the regular twelve standard bunks, nearly every cushioned surface unfolds into a bed, and there are hanging cots that fold up into the wall in the front and back lounges. It seems to be able to accommodate twenty people or more but there are only nine of us on this trip. The driver looks exactly like Santa Claus crossed with Jerry Garcia. He tells us his proper name, but I come to just call him Jerry.

After the show we pack up and begin the overnight drive to Denver. At about 3:00 a.m. we are thrown from our bunks as the bus swerves to correct its course. Wonder Kid flies out of a top bunk and crashes onto the floor. The Aussie is furious and runs up to scream at Jerry. He claims someone cut him off, but we don't see anyone else on the road. I'm pretty sure he fell asleep.

James has taken to wearing a full bear costume in his off time. He purchased it for his novelty side project band though he's barely played any shows. There have been exactly three, if I'm not mistaken: the very drunken occasion of Jim's birthday in Lawrence, the church in Philly where we met Sinbad at a Wawa after the show, and our label showcase for CMJ. All three times we doubled as his backing band as well as played our own set. There is nothing that speaks to the absurdity of touring life better than a grown man in a bear costume smoking a cigarette with a Bud Heavy in front of a tour bus.

For some reason I've grown my sideburns out into mutton chops and I look like Wolverine. I'm not really sure why I have done this. It's post my "90210 Luke Perry" straight burns phase and this must be my version of the ironic mustache in my early twenties. In the new offices of Our Manager's tiny record label they have commissioned a life-sized print of a photo of me complete with this audacious facial hair. Nobody told me they were gonna do that, and it's a disconcerting image to loom over me every time I visit. I have a fantastic Polaroid that now lives in my office of Honey White and I at our favorite dive bar back home, sitting in a horseshoe booth and smoking cigars. I don't smoke cigars but Logan did, and the smoldering accessory really works well with the Wolverine chops.

Our Manager must have gotten some kind of deal on this bus. It's only the second one we've ever had, and since we're not gonna be out for ten weeks we'll need to cut some corners to make the budget work. Still, having twice as many beds as people seems a little absurd. In a way this tour is a kind of traveling revue of the bands we've signed to our imprint label, Heroes & Villains. Part of Our Manager's grand plan to lure us to his tiny record company was to give us our own farm team, so we've signed our friends. The Anniversary from back home and Cujo's band Koufax round out the traveling circus that is stumbling its way across these United States.

I'm glad that my friends are here with us. The shows have gotten larger and the crowds have gotten younger. There are still diehards, but we don't seem to be playing for as many of our peers anymore, we may have outgrown that scene. Our popularity has been mostly word of mouth, with the help of some creative marketing from the label. The reviews have generally been shitty and the radio won't touch us with a ten-foot pole. What the industry is calling "Nu Metal" is the style of the day. But, fuck it, the shows keep getting bigger and the merch sales keep going up, even if I am feeling distant from the crowd.

The tour is sponsored by a new and controversial file-sharing website that is starting to revolutionize the industry. It's definitely cannibalizing album sales but record labels have notoriously robbed their artists for years, so who cares? The cries foul from bloated rock stars and executives are hilarious to me. Our Manager sees this for what it is, a promotional tool. The more people who hear your music, the more people will come to the show and buy a shirt. We've always made the bulk of our living through performing anyway. Besides, they are giving us a bit of scratch to help pay for the bus, and all we have to do is display a small banner by the merch.

I am at the Great American Music Hall in the Castro district of San Francisco. It's a gorgeous building with ornate architecture on the inside. Backstage there is a long hallway that is currently filled with executives and lackeys from the file-sharing website. They are all wearing matching black T-shirts with the company logo like it's some sort of corporate retreat. Who let all these tech bros back here? I decide to start doing vocal warm-ups, which I never do, and begin a series of "Me Me Mo Mo Mo's" at increasing volume and pitch. This not only overpowers their conversations but signals that it's time for them to leave so we can get ready to go onstage. They are ushered out by The Aussie as I sit back down to nurse my whiskey.

Los Angeles, House of Blues on the Sunset Strip. I truly hate this town, and I think I know why. The only places we see are this club and the Hyatt, or "Riot House," across the street. Later, I would come to learn that LA is actually a series of much smaller cities and is actually pretty bitchin', but for now all I see is this Boulevard of Broken Dreams. There is one place I like to play in this town, The Troubadour. One of the bands with us on this tour is the same one our old merch guy sings in. He finally gets to perform on this hallowed stage. He would have gotten there on his own eventually but I feel a sense of pride that we were able to help him scratch that off his bucket list.

San Diego, at Canes, a club right on the ocean. The backstage is smaller that the toilet on the bus so we all linger outside. The absolute unit that works the security here is a sight to behold. I've played here a couple times and have never seen him wear a shirt. He's a very soft spoken and gentle man, but fuck, he's intimidating. This is one of those shows that probably should have a barricade but doesn't, so he's gonna have his work cut out for him.

I've started to appreciate the barricade more than I used to. As the crowd has gotten younger they haven't gotten any less adventurous, but they are less experienced at the practice of the pit. Crowd surfing has become more common, it used to happen only on rare occasions when we started. However, these invincible youths can't seem to navigate where the crowd ends and my microphone begins, and I've been hit in the mouth more often lately. I tend to close my eyes when I sing but I've taken to standing guard during the more raucous numbers, always aware of the incoming human projectiles.

This night a young man lands on the stage after I dodge his descent. He jumps up off the floor, grabs the mic away from my reach and starts to sing the song poorly. I don't even have to look side stage for The Aussie to rush out and pull the kid offstage. At least he's not tackling them anymore, I finally talked him out of that one.

This practice is happening more and more, and it's really starting to irritate me. Not so much the sentiment, I'm fine if people want to get onstage and sing along with us. Hell, I've done it to other bands myself. It's that they don't want to sing with me, they want to sing on their own, and it fucks up the flow of the gig. I think I've always taken the professionalism of our performances seriously, but the stakes are a lot lower when it's thirty people at a five-dollar basement show. These people paid real money, enough for us to be able to afford a bus, and it wasn't to hear some rando sing the songs out of key.

I've stopped going to the merch table after shows. I've pretty much stopped going by the merch table at all unless it's before doors. Besides the strain on my voice, more people are recognizing me (must be the sideburns) and some of them are pretty intense. People are scared to talk to me (again, maybe the Wolverine chops) and when they do they often tell me really heavy shit. Things like, "your music helped me when my mom died," and though I am flattered I really don't know how to respond to that. There has been a definite shift from "we're all in this together" into a more traditional band-and-performer relationship. That wasn't something I ever expected, so I almost exclusively hang out with the other bands and our crew. At least we're all on the same page.

Houston, Texas, Fitzgerald's. We have to cancel this show because, as a favor to Our Manager, we fly to Boston to perform a radio gig for the one rock station that plays us. If it was gonna be anywhere, it would be there. I've written enough about the place, even an anthem for their highway. Local songs get you local work. At this Boston amphitheater the lineup is a then-unknown Nickleback, The Kottonmouth Kings, the all-femme Canadian goth metal outfit Kittie, and us. This is gonna be interesting. We take the stage in a cloud of marijuana smoke, and during our set it's raining beer cups and empty cigarette packs. Glad we cancelled a perfectly good show for this.

We've smoked enough weed that we are going to attempt to see if we can get Radiohead's *Kid A* to sync up with *The Nightmare Before Christmas*, à la *Dark Side Of The Moon* and *The Wizard Of Oz*. In our altered states we convince ourselves that the album perfectly lines up with the film, and then I pass out.

I wake up in the middle of the night sweating. My heart is racing, my blood sugar has obviously plummeted. I don't even have time to check it with my meter, I am in enough of a panic that I'm absolutely certain that I am in a crisis. I've only been asleep an hour or two but I am now sober as a judge and need to find sustenance. I find an orange juice in the fridge and down the twenty-ounce bottle in one breathless gulp. Then I check the freezer for any of James' chocolate, but I come up bare. He's not back from the bar yet and I know he keeps candy in his bunk, so I root around for it but, still, nothing. I then remember that we have a half-eaten bag of Doritos from the rider in one of the cupboards. Finally, success. I sit down at the small table and finish the bag, waiting for the worst to pass.

This has been something of a trial-and-error phase as far as my relationship with alcohol as a diabetic. Beer does seem to move the needle carb-wise but wine and spirits do not. You'd think wine, with all the sugar, would be incompatible, but that hasn't proven to be the case for me. I'm still finding my footing with my tolerance, and what really stirs the pot is eating late at night. If I eat straight protein or veg then I'm fine but we've started getting after-show pizzas and those make it hard to guess how much insulin to take.

This kind of blood sugar incident doesn't happen often, but if you add copious amounts of alcohol into the equation things can get messy. Honey White called an ambulance for me once because I was drunk and my blood sugar went out of whack. I was fine eventually but she was reprimanded by the EMT for letting me drink too much. It wasn't her fault, I'm just getting my sea legs is all.

There are lots of reasons why so many in our industry turn to substances. First, you work in taverns and you're encouraged to drink at work. Second, being in a band on tour is like having an extended adolescence—debauchery and bad behavior are an assumed, if not encouraged, part of the gig. Third, if you're on a bus and you're not in the crew there's fuck nothing to do all day. You're tethered to the venue by a fairly short leash since you've got to come and go for load in, sound check and showtime. Finally, at least for me, when I'm touring I feel really disconnected and lonely. I don't relate to a lot of the people at the show and I really would rather be at home with my girl.

In order to evade that looming storm cloud I start drinking with the band. Alcohol has become the tie that binds us, it's what we do when we are together. Up until the last year or so I never imbibed because I was always the sober one who would drive the van. I was the "responsible" one, I've been told. But we all played the gig, that's really our only "responsibility." I don't have to be the sober one but it's something I can control.

Especially in the madness of our earlier outings, having some sense of schedule was helpful for my anxiety. Even though I resented having to wake people up and do the bulk of the driving, it provided structure. Driving could give my brain something to do, I would calculate our potential arrival time based on the current mile marker and the speed at which I drove. When we moved up to a bus all that purpose went away. At first I was relieved, but now I'm struggling with what to do with myself.

Combine that with the relatively new realization that I can't be expected to go out after the show and still have a voice the next day, and I'm spending a lot of time alone. I try to hang with our crew, but they've got actual work to do so they don't have a lot of free time. Instead, I've taken to nursing a drink and watching cooking shows on the bus' satellite television all by myself. The glorious life of a rock star.

I'll Catch You

I'm on a pay phone outside of the cafeteria of some university in upstate New York. Shows at universities are rare and they aren't the big ticket, SUA payout sort of gig that some bands get. That's apparently a whole circuit, but we tend to either play at some club in the student union or, on occasion, in the cafeteria. This is one of those cafeteria gigs, but at least it's after hours and filled with people who want to be there. In Norman, Oklahoma, we actually played during the lunch rush to the general student population. That was awkward.

I'm on the phone with Honey White, who is back in Boston, and I am freaking out. She's been off the whole conversation, and I can tell she's keeping something from me. I finally get her to admit that my fears are correct, but she still won't tell me what it is. She swears that it isn't anything bad but she's still not going to tell me. This feels like such a betrayal to me and I tell her as much. She tells me to calm the fuck down, she's unfortunately used to this paranoia on my part. I hate surprises, even good ones, and she knows this but doesn't seem to care. I tell her that I feel like this is one of those trust-building exercises and I'm gonna fall over backwards and she's gonna drop me. "Don't worry," she says, "I'll catch you." "You'll catch me?" I ask timidly. "Yeah babe, I'll catch you."

The summer before Honey White moved to Boston we took the train to Chicago to see Jawbreaker at the Metro on the *Dear You* tour. Fluf and The Smoking Popes opened up, Josh Caterer sang their whole set while chewing gum. It was both disgusting and impressive. The Metro was like a cathedral, much larger than any punk venue I'd ever been to. The show was amazing, and the band's rumored dislike of each other was not apparent in the least. Blake held his fingers up in a "W" to signal that they were going to play "Want" at the end of the encore, and we both screamed every word. It was glorious.

We were staying at DePaul University, in the dorm room of a friend of ours who I had known since kindergarten. The night we got there, either there was a fire or someone pulled the fire alarm, but the whole building was evacuated at 2:00 a.m. as the alarms sounded. Thank fuck the sprinklers didn't go off, so our luggage was spared. We stood out in the Chicago night waiting for the building to burn, but it never did.

This was the last trip we were going to take before she left for school. We didn't travel often, usually to her grandparents' house at Lake of the Ozarks, and one time to St. Louis to see The Cure. That was another amazing show. Regardless, we both knew that at some point after this weekend things were gonna change. We had committed to the long-distance relationship concept though we both knew it was a long shot. I was banking on my persistent codependency to make the whole thing work but the fact is, I didn't want her to go. I was torn. I did want her to be happy, and I knew that going to this school had been her goal since before we met. I just wanted her to be happy with me, I wanted to be enough for her. This was, of course, unfair. As long as I was driven to make music and tour, she was never going to be enough for me either.

I thought taking the train would be romantic, but I'm afraid the Southern Eagle from Kansas City to Chicago and back is a more utilitarian affair. The trains are ravaged by abuse and disrepair, it's not exactly the golden age of rail travel. Regardless of this, going to the city to see one of our favorite bands at a mythical venue made for a very magical weekend. When Jawbreaker broke up a little while later I hoped it didn't mean that Honey and I would break up too. I wouldn't let it.

My desire to tour was established before Honey White moved to Boston. I don't know when my ambition evolved from just wanting to play music to wanting to travel while I did it. It may have been in high school, after the experience of seeing national touring acts at The Rhumba Box, or after Boys Life and Giant's Chair proved to me it was possible. The Dischord work ethic had always been my North Star, and then I saw that some local boys were able to do it, too. I knew it was something that I could pull off, or at least something that I had to try.

It was Honey White's departure that widened the scope of my vision. I'd known some bands that did the I-35 circuit from Minneapolis down to Austin every few months. Others would do the I-70/I-55 loop through Columbia, St. Louis, Chicago and Milwaukee, with the occasional stop in Champaign or Madison. In order for me to get to Boston to see my girl, we were going to have to go nationwide. You can't really drive to the Northeast for a weekender on a regular basis unless you're a madman. Therefore we were gonna have to find places to play along the way. There were a hundred different ways to play your way to Boston and back, and I was gonna do them all as often as I could.

After our difficult phone call I sulk back to the show. You wouldn't know my anxious mood, at least not onstage. I've learned that channeling any of those fears into the set makes for a good show. I leap into the air more often than usual, pounding the guitar until my fingers bleed. I scream the words that are already fraught with insecurity even before I inject my current unhappiness into them. If anything, the crowd is better off for my suffering, it seems to make me a better performer.

A few days after the phone call, we are headlining our own show at The Metro in Chicago. Our original haunt had been the Fireside Bowl but when we outgrew that most precious of clubs we moved up to The Metro. The first time we played here I was terrified, having built up the image of the place in my mind from the Jawbreaker show. First off, the stage is enormous compared to what we're used to, and the club has a balcony. What are we, the ballet?

The room is both ornate and cavernous, yet somehow intimate and just dirty enough to keep it from being sterile. The music we play is best suited to a certain level of squalor. A sterile environment feels too corporate and bloated. The trade off is that often the backstage conditions for the band can also be pretty disgusting. Not at The Metro, where the green rooms are clean and free of graffiti. Posters for classic shows from the past adorn the walls, and they've already got a pot of coffee brewing. It's the best of both worlds.

We're on in twenty minutes so I try to call Honey White, she'll probably be in bed before we get offstage so I want to say goodnight. She doesn't pick up, and I worry. We haven't spoken since this morning, which is relatively uncommon as I usually check in with her a couple times a day. This is obsessive, I know, but it's the pattern we've established.

We take the stage in front of a sold-out crowd and launch into the first song, "I'm A Loner Dottie, a Rebel." This is one of the few times I've attempted to write lyrics from someone else's perspective. There are plenty of songs about other people, but this is the first one where I inhabit a different individual. It couldn't be any less me. The song is about a one-night stand that a friend had, and thus the immortal line from Pee Wee Herman became the title even though it doesn't appear in the song. It's the kind of '80s pop cultural reference that will be somewhat hack in the coming years but right now still feels fresh, at least to me.

There was some controversy when this song came out. It was originally released on a split 7" with Braid on our first tour together. Some thought the subject matter was misogynistic, but that was misguided. The song is about two consenting adults who are having a fairly mature discussion about whether or not they want to make the previous evening into a broader relationship, and ultimately deciding that they don't want to. That some people thought I was singing about myself was also hilariously inaccurate. I'm way too obsessed with Honey White to even glance at anyone else.

We've started letting the crowd take the lead on the opening line of the song. They erupt after the drum fill that starts the number, and they wait patiently during the ridiculously long instrumental intro. Jim and I walk to the front of the stage away from the microphones and throw our index fingers in the air, signaling that "you guys are gonna take it from here." The band drops out, only Jim's guitar keeping the rhythm. The entire room explodes in unison, screaming the first line, the lyrical foundation of the song, and we've got them. I can read the energy of any room, and if I have any question that they aren't with us then I'll sing the line myself. Only on rare occasions have I misread the crowd and given them the solo only to be met with silence. There's nothing more embarrassing than attempting an arena rock move and having it fall flat.

Tonight, though, the audience is on our side. They know every song from our first record as well as the EP that preceded it. To be honest, I don't even have to sing. We could just be the instrumental accompaniment to their collective karaoke, but instead I feed off their enthusiasm and match it with my own. We walk offstage and pant and sweat and re-up on beverages. The backstage is downstairs so we have to hurry down to use the bathroom and freshen our cocktails. We could Axl Rose it and wait until we're damn good and ready and nobody would leave. But our collective anxiety doesn't allow for this, we need to get back out there ASAP.

We walk back out onstage and I thank the crowd and the venue and the opening bands, and decide to tell the story of the Jawbreaker show from years before. I let the crowd know how meaningful this club is to me from that memory. It's at this point that I glance to the side of the stage and lay my eyes on Honey White, in the flesh, all the way from Boston. She had planned the elaborate surprise for weeks, borrowing money from her soon-to-be estranged father and communicating with the band to keep it a secret. It's the last night of the tour, and she's gonna ride home with us and spend the weekend with me. I'm filled with shock and happiness and relief. I want to throw off my guitar and grab her, but she waves me off. She knows we have to finish the show first. The two-song encore feels like fifteen seconds and I run to the side of the stage and into her embrace.

A few weeks later I am at a catering company tasting wedding cake. Cake tasting is not something that diabetics normally do, but since I only intend to get married once in my life I figure it's ok this one time. Planning the wedding has been a bit of a battle with mothers who want to be more involved, or have more say in the guest list, but since they aren't contributing financially I feel like it's our call to make. We've got the venue sorted, The Simpson House in Kansas City. The officiant is going to be Wonder Kid, since he got ordained by The Universal Life Church online. James is gonna take care of the music on the baby grand piano that comes with the space. The biggest expense is procuring enough alcohol to satiate our friends and tour mates.

As a way to offset the expense of several of our friends' bands coming to town for the ceremony, a show is organized at The Bottleneck. After the corn field strip club hedonism of The Outhouse previously mentioned, and the Arthur Bryant's BBQ-stuffed rehearsal dinner at our favorite dive bar, we're pretty loose on the way to the show. I originally wanted us to perform, but the difficult logistics of that bad idea quickly became apparent. There's kind of a strange atmosphere here since our whole band, our friends, and our friends' bands are here for a bachelor / bachelorette party, but there are still paying customers at the show. They must be wondering what all the celebration is about, but people around here have to come to learn that we really only do anything for fun in this town, so maybe they're used to it.

The show is a messy, drunken success, and I bid my love farewell since we're not supposed to see each other in the morning. She's going to her mother's, and I'm going back to our place to wind down with one of our early wedding gifts. The Anniversary have gifted us a nine-pack of beer, since they drank three of them after they put a bow on the case. Classy lot, them.

The next morning I feel like death and race to make coffee and find something greasy to fill my tortured stomach. I am only twenty-three, so hangovers still don't really last that long, and besides I am all endorphins and fear for the day ahead. At the Simpson House, I coordinate with the caterers while Honey White gets ready upstairs. I'm already dressed in my wedding suit and am barking orders like a military general.

People have started to show, mostly the blue-haired set, including my grandmother, so I send James to the piano. He plays a mix of random hotel lobby melodies and songs by the bands in attendance, all of whom are wearing ill-fitting thrift store suits purchased earlier in the day. They look like they work at WKRP in Cincinnati. I take my place next to Wonder Kid as James launches into our wedding march, "Faded" by The Afghan Whigs.

The ceremony is short, about ninety seconds in all. That part was really a formality, we just wanted to have a party and so that's what we do. After several hours of small talk and thanking people for coming, I slip outside with some of the attendees to smoke a joint on the lawn. Honey White is pissed that she can't join us, her gown making her the most conspicuous person here, but ultimately she's just glad it's over. We've made it through the day.

We're driven back to our hotel, where we collapse in exhaustion, taking time only to open a card from Mr. Happy. The card reads "I'm sorry for your loss" and includes a check for one hundred and sixty-two dollars and seventeen cents. My new wife asks me what the significance of that figure is, but I have no idea. There's so much about that guy that I don't know. Hell, tonight was the only time I've ever seen him without a hat.

When the dust finally settles the enormity starts to dawn on us. We're married, husband and wife, the first of our friends who have done this. The only married people we know outside of our parents. We both feel good about the decision, but it is a little weird, let alone that we'll both be getting used to wearing a ring all the time. We talk about the future. I'm gonna be leaving on tour again in a little over a month and I don't think either of us really realized just how soon that is. We only had our eyes on this particular prize, the wedding.

The reality that I've convinced her to move here, and will then be turning around and leaving, is starting to sink in. She doesn't have a job here, and doesn't have many friends outside of the band's social circle. Those people treat her like "my girlfriend," or I guess now "my wife," rather than a fully formed human in her own right. Nobody is suggesting that I stop touring, that would be madness. The band is still on an upward trajectory that shows no sign of stopping. I'm making more money than we know what to do with, so she really doesn't have to work if she doesn't want to. But, what kind of a life is that? Not one that she wants, that's for sure.

We are at a crossroads, but I am unable to see it. I am so focused and dedicated to my career that even though what we both want is for me to be at home, it doesn't seem like something that I can do. I've entered into this weird tax bracket where I'm not really qualified to do any other job. I'm certainly never going to earn this much doing something else. Best to keep on truckin', I tell her. She reluctantly agrees with me and starts trying to figure out her life in this sleepy college hamlet.

About the author

Matt Pryor is the frontman for the longrunning acts The Get Up Kids and The New Amsterdams as well as an accomplished solo artist. His first book *Red Letter Days* is an intimate glimpse into his life from 1990–2000. "This was never meant to be a book about emo or even the band in particular, I didn't want to write about the 'scene.' That is already well documented," he explains. "I just wanted to write a book to see if I could do it. It's the same way I felt when I was sixteen and I wanted to make an album: I don't really have a reason, it's just something I wanted to do."

The result is a collection of short vignettes about Pryor's early life, his struggle with childhood Diabetes and what it was like crisscrossing the country (and the continents) with his band in the days before iPhones and texting. It's a snapshot of a time period that feels nostalgic yet familiar. "Every one of the stories in the book is one that I've told backstage, at a bar or on a porch," Pryor says. "I just wanted to translate them from an oral tradition to a written one." From playing shows in nontraditional venues to detailing the cast of characters he meets along the way, *Red Letter Days* gives insight into how Pryor processed this time period through first-person accounts of his most memorable moments.

"I have found—and this is fairly recently—that things I write don't really hit me like that until later," Pryor responds when asked about how it felt to revisit this era on an emotional level. "In the moment I just think that's a cool song, lyric or story; it seems to be that I can only really connect on that level once I've had some distance from it." Whether you were at one of those sweaty all ages shows in the '90s or have only discovered his music recently, *Red Letter Days* is a document of that era told in a conversational tone that is as entertaining as it is endearing.

Published by
Washed Up Books
Los Angeles, CA

www.washedupbooks.com

All rights reserved
All text © 2023 Matt Pryor

First edition
© 2023 Washed Up Emo, LLC

No part of this book may
be used or reproduced in
any manner without written
permission of the publisher,
except in the context of
reviews.

Every reasonable attempt has
been made to identify owners
of copyright. Errors or
omissions will be corrected in
subsequent editions.

Edited by Ian King
Produced by Tom Mullen
Designed by Jesse Reed, Order
Proofread by Elisabeth Dahl
Author bio by Jonah Bayer

Cover photo by
Nathan Houbraken

Back cover photo by
Michael Dubin

ISBN 979-8-218-22889-7

Printed in the USA

Washed Up Books is distributed
by Polyvinyl Records
Champaign, IL

For wholesale inquiries
please contact:
retail@polyvinylrecords.com

Special thanks:
Matt Wilson, Michael Dubin,
Paul Drake, Chris Hassen,
Matt Lunsford, Chelsea Hodson,
Hector Silva, Amanda Pitts,
Jonah Bayer, Ian King, and
Nathan Houbraken.

Type:
Schmalfette
Chronicle Text G3
Pitch Sans

Photo credits:
8   Paul Drake
30   Denea Mesa
48   Michael Dubin
66   Michael Dubin
84   Paul Drake
98   Paul Drake
120   Paul Drake
142   Michael Dubin
170   Christine Kosirog
188   Michael Dubin
208   Paul Drake

WashedUp
Books